THE PRENTICE HALL G   ~TO

EVALUATI
ONLINE RESOURCES
WITH
RESEARCH NAVIGATOR

CRIMINAL JUSTICE
2004

Melissa Payton
with contributions by Laura Joyce

PEARSON
Prentice
Hall

UPPER SADDLE RIVER, NJ 07458

©2004 by PEARSON EDUCATION, INC.
Upper Saddle River, New Jersey 07458

ISBN 0-13-184460-1

Printed in the United States of America

Note: Research Navigator™ is continually expanded and updated. The screen shots included in this documentation may not reflect the latest updates. Refer to <http://www.researchnavigator.com/phguide/> to download the most recent documentation in either Microsoft® Word format or Adobe Acrobat® format.

Contents

Chapter 1

An Overview of Sources

What Are Sources?

When instructors speak of sources, they're usually referring to "outside" sources--materials outside your own knowledge or thinking that contain someone else's ideas. Sources provide information; they let you learn something you did not know before. Examples of legitimate sources include credible information from the Internet, library collections, and the spoken words of experts. They can be in the form of books, newspaper articles, interviews, television and radio programs, websites, maps, online databases, magazines, computer and video images, audiotapes, and academic journals. Sources add authority to what you write and nearly all college research assignments require their use.

Using sources well is the hallmark of sound nonfiction writing. Most research writing involves a combination of print and online sources. Although this guide will focus on online resources, the advice on evaluating sources--determining whether a website offers credible information that meets the standards of academic research--almost always applies to other sources as well.

 Later chapters will help you use sources effectively in your writing. Chapter 2 will help you find online sources, use databases and search engines, and evaluate such sources for credibility. While the Internet is a nearly bottomless well of useful and enlightening information, it is also host to websites created by bigots, conspiracy theorists, and extremists--not to mention those who are well-intentioned but misinformed. Chapter 2 will help you sort the academically nutritious wheat from the Internet junk-food chaff.

Chapter 3 will help you avoid plagiarism, a cardinal sin. It will also acquaint you with paraphrasing and summarizing, and how to cite and document sources. Chapter 4 will introduce you to Research Navigator, a new online academic research service, and Chapters 5, 6, and 7 will show you how to use the service's three major databases. Chapter 8 will help you to use Research Navigator in a specific academic discipline.

Primary and Secondary Sources

Primary sources are firsthand evidence, based on your own or someone else's original work or direct observation. They can be documents, records, letters, diaries, novels, poems, short stories, autobiographies, interviews, and journals. This original quality adds to a source's reliability and impact on the reader.

Here is playwright Endesha Ida Mae Holland in her memoir, "From the Mississippi Delta" (1997):

> I was born into the double shotgun house at 114 East Gibb Street. Mama rented both sides of the clapboard house, which stood on raised posts. A confused patch of petunias hugged the ground at the end of the front porch. Inside, the crudely painted walls were peeling and patched with newspaper. The ceiling was so low that I could read "Little Lulu" on the funny pages pasted there. (pp. 19-20)

Holland goes on to describe the cracks in the linoleum floor that offered a view of the earth under the house and the patched roof that let in daylight and rain. Her brief account does more than describe a house: it tells us, indirectly but powerfully, about the poverty she was born into.

Secondary sources report, describe, comment on, or analyze the experiences or work of others. In college, most textbooks are secondary sources. As a piece of evidence, a secondary source is at least once removed from the primary source. It reports on the original work, the direct observation, or the firsthand experience. But it can have great value and impact as a source if the reporter or writer is reliable, either as a result of special experience (a journalist who spent years observing and reporting on the civil rights movement) or special training (a tooth-decay expert with a dental degree).

Newspapers are typical secondary sources. In a three-part series the *New York Times* published in January, 2003, reporters who examined the safety record of an Alabama-based pipe-making company concluded that it was "one of the most dangerous businesses in America." They based their conclusion on primary sources: company and government records and interviews with current and former employees, including plant managers, safety directors, and environmental engineers.

Here is a quote from the story:

> "The people, they're nothing," said Robert S. Rester, a former McWane plant manager who spoke at length about his 24 years with the company. "They're just numbers. You move them in and out. I mean, if they don't do the job, you fire them. If they get hurt, complain about safety, you put a bull's-eye on them." (Barstow & Bergman, Jan. 9, 2003, p. A1)

The *Times*, and most newspapers and magazines, are generally reliable secondary sources--although even highly-regarded publications make errors under the pressure of deadlines or competition. That's why sound research requires more than one source to back up a disputable claim.

Types of Sources

Print Sources

Newspapers, magazines, academic journals, documents, reference works, and personal papers are all print sources, although more and more of them exist in an online form as well.

For college research, the main tool for locating print sources that are not online is still the library. Many times you'll need to use electronic resources, especially the library catalog, to locate the print materials that you need to pull from the library's shelves. One major advantage of libraries: they come equipped with librarians. Reference-desk staffers can help you home in on the topic you need to research, come up with a research strategy, and determine the best tools to use in your research. The "Using Your Library" section of Research Navigator can also help you use a library's vast resources more efficiently.

Online and Database Sources

The Internet offers unlimited opportunities for research. Many print sources--newspapers, magazines, reference works, academic journals--are available online as well. One advantage of accessing print sources online, of course, is that you have millions of pages originating from across the globe at your fingertips. Another is that you can download and print a copy of an article for your files. Finally, many online-print sources are *searchable*: you can type a keyword into an archive or database to pull up the page you need. (Databases collect and organize content online so that users can find particular information. When did the "The Wizard of Oz" debut, and how many Oscars did it win? The Internet Movie Database, www.imdb.com, will tell you. Searching online databases is a skill of its own that will be covered in the next chapter.)

Online content that is *not* print-based is even more varied. The most useful sites for research usually are informational and have URL addresses that end in **.edu** or **.gov**. "Edu" websites are sponsored by educational institutions, and they may include research results, reference works, subject indexes, and databases useful in many disciplines. "Gov" sites, sponsored by government agencies, offer a trove of primary sources: census information, federal codes and regulations, licensing records, property data, and health statistics. Sites that end in **.org** are sponsored by a nonprofit organization, such as Planned Parenthood, the National Rifle Association, or Mothers Against Drunk Driving. Some "org" sites offer reliable, usable information--but remember that they are usually sponsored by a group or individual that seeks to influence public opinion.

Although most commercial sites (those with **.com** URLs) exist to sell merchandise, some do offer information useful to students and researchers at low or no cost. News sites are an example (www.nytimes.com, www.newsweek.com, www.washingtonpost.com). Most offer free access to at least the previous week's content. Unfortunately, more and more publications are charging for access to their archives--which contain the information most useful for research. Many college departments, however, buy a subscription to fee-charging online publications like the *Wall Street Journal* or news databases like LexisNexus. You will need to get a sign-on and password from your instructor or department office. (The online Research Navigator, www.researchnavigator.com, free with the purchase of any Prentice Hall college textbook, allows one-year access to the *New York Times*, along with searchable databases of academic and general interest publications and World Wide Web sites.)

Chapter 2

How to Find and Evaluate Online Sources

Finding Online Sources

Yes, there is a wealth of information on the Internet. In fact no one knows how many World Wide Web pages exist, because new ones are being created constantly--they number in the millions, certainly, and some say billions. But how do you find the information you need? And how do you make sure it is credible? Anyone with a few technical skills and access to a computer can publish on the Internet. Some sites offer information from experts; many sites are run by amateurs. Some sites are updated frequently; others, not at all.

To search the Web efficiently, it helps to be familiar with several different strategies and use the one that works best for your research topic. The two main vehicles for accessing information through the Internet are **subject directories** and **search engines**, which will be discussed in more detail in this chapter. If you try out several examples of both types, you will quickly find the search method you favor. Also, search engines and subject directories are not uniform in the techniques users must employ to narrow or broaden a search. So if you are comfortable with several methods of searching--using Boolean operators, truncation (or wild cards), and implied operators, also explained in this chapter-- you will be able to switch more easily from one search engine or subject directory to another.

Strategies for Searching the Web

Tailor your search to the scope of the information you are seeking. To do this, you will need to understand **search engines**, **subject directories**, and **specialized databases**. A subject directory will take you through a sequence of Internet subjects. You might start with "history," move to "military history," then to "Civil War history," "Civil War battles," and arrive finally at the Battle of Gettysburg, your goal. Internet search engines locate specific Internet sites devoted to your topic (such as Military History Online's "Battle of Gettysburg" site). They often feature both subject directories and keyword searches.

5

Specialized databases, which usually search a targeted topic or aspect of a topic, are sometimes hard to find with search engines, but there are websites that specialize in collecting links to them. All three of these types of searching tools are explained in greater detail later in this chapter.

The two most popular organizers of Web content are probably Yahoo! (www.yahoo.com) and Google (www.google.com). Google is known mainly for its search engine, admired by many for the way it produces highly relevant results. Google does offer other services (discussion forums, a subject directory, and news sources) and is regularly adding new ones. Yahoo!, which is older, is known more as a Web **portal**, or a site that offers a range of resources and services, including e-mail, on-line shopping, games, and chat forums. As an information resource, Yahoo! was once identified with its subject directory, in contrast to Google's search engine. But in recent years, Yahoo! has added a search engine. In 2002, Yahoo!'s search engine--and others--began using Google's database in response to Google's popularity, as well as to criticism that Yahoo! search results could be influenced by advertisers who paid for inclusion in its database. Both Google and Yahoo! now accept commercial listings, but they are identified as "sponsored links" or "sponsored matches" and grouped separately, usually at the top of the first results page. Use caution when considering using any information from a site seeking to sell a product (see "Evaluating Online Sources," later in this chapter).

Subject Directories

For general, research-oriented queries, for browsing, and to view sites recommended by experts, use a subject directory. There are two basic types: academic and professional directories, which are most useful to researchers, and commercial portals that cater to the general public.

Here are some commercial portals:

- **About.com**   www.about.com
- **Go.network**   www.go.com
- **Lycos**   www.lycos.com
- **Yahoo!**   www.yahoo.com

For example, in early 2003, Yahoo!'s homepage featured 14 major categories as links to further information. Clicking on "Health" would take you to another page, with dozens more subcategories. Clicking on the subcategory "Teen Health" resulted in links to 60 websites on the subject. They ranged from a government site aimed at helping girls become "fit for life" to a men's magazine site that emphasized selling products as much as offering advice. Yahoo! and other commercial sites do not evaluate user-submitted content when adding Web pages to a database; they leave the evaluation up to the user.

Academic directories, on the other hand, are often annotated by experts and are usually the result of much thought and care. To get started on finding such directines, try the University of Albany list of Internet Subject Directories (http://library.albany.edu/internet/subject.html). Other suggestions:

- **The Librarians' Index to the Internet** (www.lii.org). Sometimes called "the thinking person's Yahoo!."
- **The WWW Virtual Library** (www.vlib.org). One of the oldest and most respected subject directories on the Web. Many of the individual subject collections are maintained at universities.
- **INFOMINE** (infomine.ucr.edu). Compiled by the University of California at Riverside.

Search Engines

For targeted and complex queries, use a search engine. A search engine does not search the entire Internet; it searches **databases,** or collections of logically-related information, that are developed by the company hosting the search engine. That's why different search engines will produce different results. There are at least two ways for a page to be recorded in the search engine's database: the page's publisher can register it with the engine, or the search engine can use software called "spiders" to search the Internet and gather information that is then recorded in the engine's database.

Search engines may offer both subject directories and keyword searches. With most search engines, you enter your search terms and click on a "go" button or hit your return key. Then the engine generates a page with links to resources containing all or some of your terms. The resources are usually ranked by term: that is, one will rank higher if your search term appears many times, near the beginning of the document, in the title, and so forth.

A fairly recent development is a "second-generation" search engine, such as Google, which ranks Web pages according to the number of pages that link to them. This strategy adds an element of human judgment---in essence, it ranks a site by how popular it is--to computer technology. Many users start with Google, even for general queries, because it does such an excellent job of finding relevant documents.

Some popular search engines are:

- **AltaVista**   altavista.digital.com/
- **Excite**   www.excite.com
- **Google**   www.google.com/
- **Hotbot**   www.hotbot.com
- **Webcrawler**   www.webcrawler.com

Your choice of keywords to launch the search is just as important as your choice of search engine. Use the words you would like to find in the title, description, or text of an Internet site. Searching for a common or general word, such as "Clinton," will provide a massive search of every document that contains this term. (The lowercase **clinton** will find both upper- and lower-case instances of the term.) In fact, **clinton** generated 6.9 million results from Google, ranging from Hillary Clinton's official Senate Web page, to a biography of President Clinton, to a Clinton County, Mich., government site--all on the first results page. You'll get more usable results by narrowing your query. Do you want a biography of President Clinton? Clinton's stand on a particular issue? A chronology of Clinton's impeachment trial? Using more than one keyword will narrow your results and make them more relevant to your needs; even with thousands of results, most search engines will put the most relevant pages at the top of the results list.

It's also possible to conduct too narrow a search. If you combine keywords for something like "Ulysses S. Grant's military strategy at Gettysburg," you may produce few or no results. Try dropping one or more keywords until you get a usable list of links.

A **metasearch engine**, instead of creating its own database of information, searches the databases of several search engines. For example, when you enter a query at the Mamma.com website, the engine simultaneously queries about ten of the major search engines, such as Yahoo!, Webcrawler, and Magellan. It then provides you with a short, relevant list of results. **President Clinton impeachment** generated 62 results from Mamma.com, from search engines Teoma, Ask Jeeves, MSN.com, and others. Results included primary sources such as government documents and secondary sources such as press coverage--a mixture that might be useful in writing a college paper.

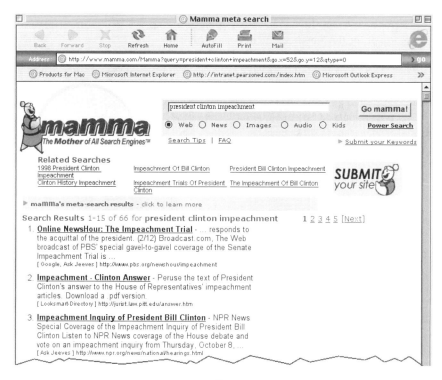

Ixquick is particularly helpful if your topic is obscure or if you want to retrieve results from several search engines without generating an enormous list. Ixquick returns only the top ten relevancy-ranked results from the source search services.

Some popular metasearch engines:

- **Ixquick** www.ixquick.com
- **ProFusion** www.profusion.com
- **Dogpile** www.dogpile.com
- **Mamma.com** www.mamma.com
- **Metacrawler.com** www.metacrawler.com

Using Boolean Terms
and Other Search Limiters

When you use a search engine, you increase your chances of getting good results by formulating a precise query. Sometimes one word (or keyword) is sufficient, if it is distinctive enough.

Many times you can click on an advanced search option that will bring up a template to prompt you through the process. But sometimes it is helpful to know Boolean logic in order to narrow your search for manageable results.

Boolean logic comes from the ideas of British mathematician George Boole (1815-1864). From his writings come the Boolean operators: AND, OR, and NOT, used to link words and phrases for more precise queries for search engines and directories.

Increasingly, search engines are simplifying their search protocols by making "and" the default logic. If you type **president clinton impeachment** in most search engines, you will get results for the equivalent of **president** AND **clinton** AND **impeachment**.

Be sure to capitalize Boolean operators; some, but not all, search engines, will assume lowercase "and" or "or" to be part of a phrase and consider them "stop" words to be ignored. (Stop words are prepositions, articles, conjunctions, and other common words like **I, an, the, for**.) Most sites offer a link to a page that explains their defaults and other search protocols. From Google's homepage, for example, click on "Advanced Search" and then "Advanced Search Tips" to find this page:

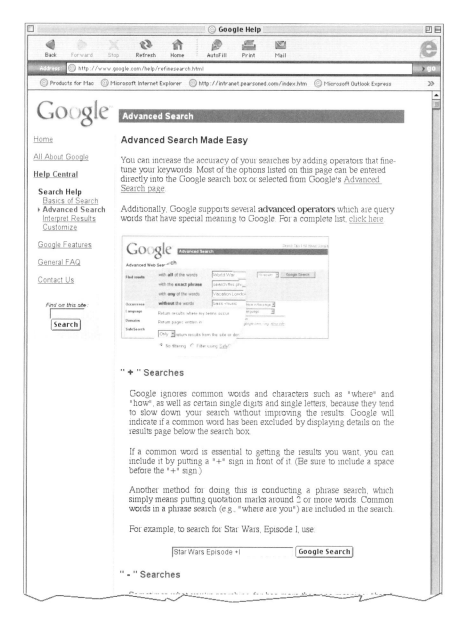

Boolean AND, OR, and NOT

The Boolean AND narrows your search by retrieving only documents that contain every one of the keywords you enter. The more terms you enter, the narrower your search becomes. Examples:

- gene AND therapy
- gene AND therapy AND risks

An Altavista search of **gene AND therapy** turned up more than 339,000 results; **gene AND therapy AND risks** generated 48,000.

10

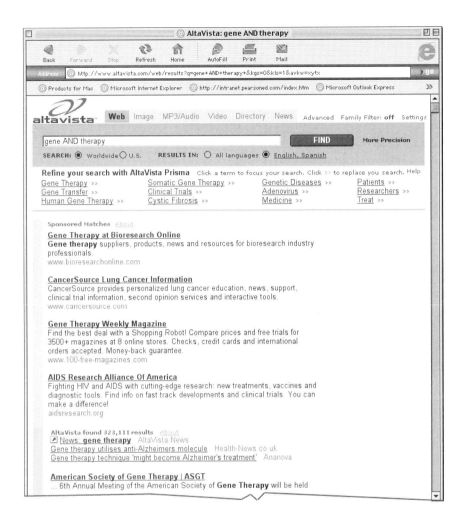

The Boolean OR expands your search by returning documents in which either or both keywords appear. Since the OR operator is usually used for keywords that are similar or synonymous, the more keywords you enter, the more documents you will retrieve. If you do a Google search of two keywords using OR and AND, you will see how OR broadens your search while AND narrows it:

- sea lions OR walruses (192,000 results)
- sea lions AND walruses (6,250 results)

The Boolean NOT or AND NOT limits your search by returning documents with only your first keyword but not the second, even if the first word appears in that document, too. For example, if you type in **seals** as a keyword, you'll get many results about Easter Seals. But if you wanted information on the animal, you could type:

- seals NOT Easter
- seals AND NOT Easter

Many search engines convert formal Boolean operators into more user-friendly template terminology when you enter their advanced search pages. The Google advanced search template gives you these options:

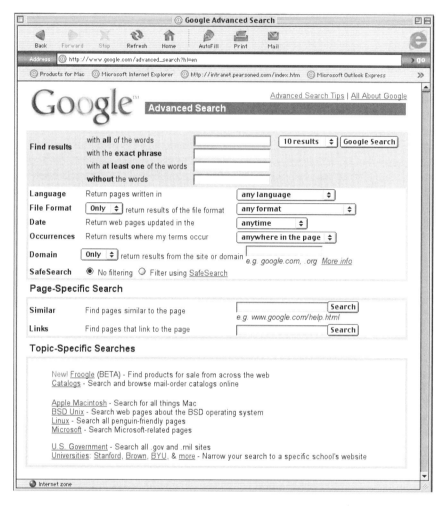

In the template above, "all the words" is equivalent to the Boolean AND; "at least one of the words," the Boolean OR; and "without the words," the Boolean NOT. "Exact phrase" means that if you type in **President Clinton,** you will get pages where **Clinton** is always preceded by **President**; if you use the "all the words" option and type **President Clinton**, you'll get pages with **President** and **Clinton**, but not necessarily together as a phrase.

Implied and Other Non-Boolean Limiters

While full Boolean operators are accepted in the advanced search option of some search engines, "implied" Boolean operators--or what some call "search engine math"--are accepted in the basic search options of an increasing number of search engines.

Implied Boolean operators use the plus (+) symbol for AND:

- gene +therapy +risks

The implied Boolean operator for NOT is a minus (-) symbol. Typing a (+) or (-) sign in front of a word will force the inclusion or exclusion of that word in the search statement.

- pinnipeds -walruses
- Star Wars Episode +I

Search engines have different rules about spacing before and after plus or minus signs. Google specifies a space before the symbol and no space after.

The "plus" technique is helpful when a key part of your search term is normally a stop word that a search engine would ignore. For example, typing **Star Wars Episode I** into Google will return results about all Star Wars episodes because Google will eliminate the "I" as a common word. Adding "+I" will return results only about Episode I.

Implied Boolean operators have no symbol for OR. A few search engines default to OR when two terms are searched (**war battle**), but most default to AND.

Quotation Marks

In most search engines, you can use quotation marks around two or more words to make them one unit (although proper names usually do not need quotation marks).

- "gene therapy risks"
- "SUV gas mileage"

Other Limiters

Proximity, or positional, operators--ADJ, for adjacent, or NEAR--are not really part of Boolean logic, but they serve a similar function in formulating search statements. Not all search engines accept proximity operators, but a few accept NEAR in their advanced search option. The NEAR operator allows you to search for terms situated within a specified distance of each other in any order. The closer they are, the higher the document appears in the results list. Using NEAR, when possible, in place of the Boolean AND usually returns more relevant results.

- sea lions NEAR pinnipeds
- Cheney NEAR Bush

With some search engines, you can truncate the word: use its root, followed by an asterisk, to retrieve variants of the word. For example, if you can't remember whether the organization is called Feminine Majority or Feminist Majority, you can enter **femini*** to find the site you want. This is also referred to as using a wild card or "stemming." Yahoo! supports wild card searches, but Google does not; if you don't get the results you want with one form of the word in Google, try the other (**walrus OR walruses**).

Another useful technique with some search engines is **field limiting,** which limits searches to a specified part of a page: title, URL, link, host, domain, image, or text, for example. Type in the field followed by a colon. If you wanted to make sure "multiple sclerosis" was in the title of a page in order to call up only sites devoted to the topic, you'd search for **title: multiple sclerosis**. Google uses "allintitle" for a title search, so a search for **allintitle: multiple sclerosis** would yield these results:

Online Databases

Much of the World Wide Web is not directly searchable from most search engines--the information is so specialized or constantly changing that it is "invisible" to the software that search engines use to access databases. These databases are often referred to as the "invisible Web" or "deep Web." Yet information stored in these databases is accessible if you know how to find it.

Some search engines and portals help by offering separate search options for the kinds of dynamically changing information, such as job listings and news, that search engines normally can't find. Yahoo's HotJobs (hotjobs.yahoo.com) and Google's news site (news.google.com) are examples of specialized search functions separate from the company's main search engine. Some sites also offer search options for multimedia and image files (Google's Image Search), and files created in non-standard file types such as Portable Document Format (PDF).

There are websites that specialize in collecting links to databases available on the Web. One such site is called The Invisible Web (www.invisibleweb.com) and links to 10,000 Web-accessible databases.

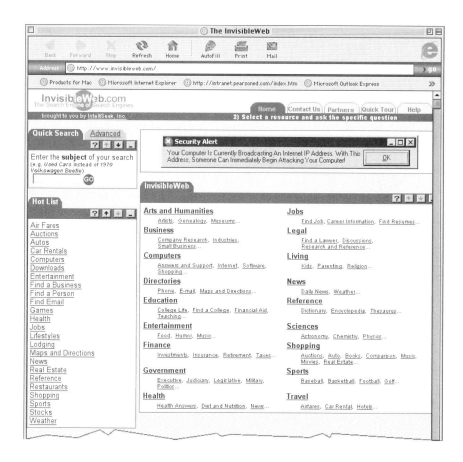

You may also want to visit other sites that collect links to Web databases:

- **Resource Discovery Network**   www.rdn.ac.uk
- **ProFusion**   www.profusion.com
- **Complete Planet**   www.completeplanet.com
- **Geniusfind**   geniusfind.com

Strategies for Searching Online Databases

Google and other search engines can locate searchable databases by searching a subject term and the word "database." For example, type **aviation accidents database** in Google, and you will get thousands of results, including a federal government database with information from 1962 and later about civil aviation accidents in the United States.

16

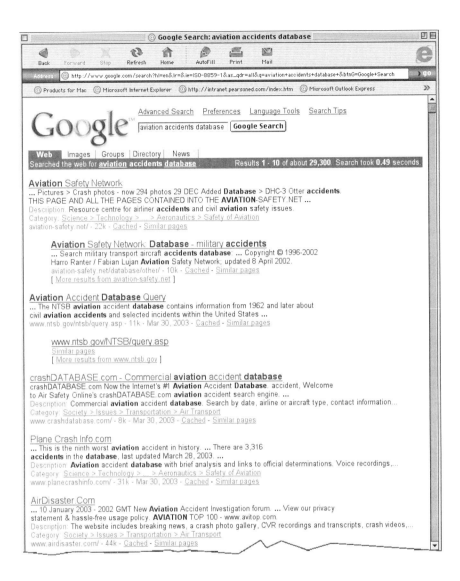

The word **database** is also helpful in searching a topic in Yahoo!, because Yahoo! uses the term to describe searchable databases in its listings. Examples:

- U.S. presidential election results database
- languages database
- toxic chemicals database

Such databases, especially if they are sponsored by government sites (identified by the **.gov** at the end of the URL), can be extremely useful as primary sources.

Planning a Search Strategy

The University of California at Berkeley has come up with a checklist (http://www.lib.berkeley.edu/TeachingLib/Guides/Internet/Strategies.html) to help you plan your search strategy. The first step is to analyze your topic to decide where to begin. Then you pick the right starting point depending on your analysis:

- If it has a distinctive word or phrase ("Battle of Gettysburg"), enclose the phrase in double quotation marks and test-run it in Google. Or search the broader concept in a subject directory.

- If it has *no* distinctive words or phrases, use more than one term or a phrase in double quotes to get fewer results from a search engine. Or try to find distinctive terms in subject directories.

- If you want an overview ("energy conservation"), look for a specialized subject directory on your topic.

- If you're seeking a narrow aspect of a broad or common topic (the role of governors in death-row pardons), try AltaVista's advanced search (www.altavista.com) or look for a directory focused on the broad subject (capital punishment).

- If your topic has synonyms (sea lion or pinniped), equivalent terms (energy conservation or fuel conservation), variant spellings (Thelonious Monk or Thelonius Monk), or endings that need to be included, choose engines with Boolean logic or truncation.

- If you don't even know where to start--you're confused and need more information--look for a gateway page or subject guide (Research Navigator's Link Library, www.researchnavigator.com), try an encyclopedia in a virtual library (the Internet Public Library, www.ipl.org), or ask at a library reference desk.

Then, stay flexible: learn as you go and vary your approach with what you learn. Don't get bogged down in a strategy that doesn't work. Switch from search engines to directories and vice versa. Find specialized directories on your topic and possible databases.

Evaluating Online Sources

In your career as a student and eventually as a professional, you will spend a great deal of time using the Internet to communicate and find information. But can you trust the information you find?

Suppose you come across two arguments regarding the greenhouse gas effect and global warming. Here are the views of a scientist who believes there is little or no greenhouse gas effect:

> Although thermometers located at Earth's surface indicate that the planet's average temperature is higher today by about 1°F than it was 140 years ago, satellite measurements of the temperature of the atmosphere thousands of feet above the surface indicate little or no warming since 1979. The difference between temperatures aloft and at the surface is not predicted by computer climate models. Therefore these models cannot be relied upon to project future warming, and the surface warming itself may be an artifact caused by urban heat islands rather than a true global warming trend.

Here is the response of an environmental organization that believes global warming is human-caused and a real threat to the environment:

> The method of translation of the satellite data into temperatures has been revised several times as errors were found and it is still not clear that these data provide a reliable means to determine long term trends. At higher altitudes, temperatures fluctuate more than at the surface due to natural climate influences like sunlight-reflecting particles from volcanoes. This variability or noise in the satellite record obscures the warming trend due to the buildup of the greenhouse gases, which is apparent in the global surface temperature data.

Which is more credible, the dissident scientist or the environmental organization? The organization also cites scientific research to back up its arguments. Because experts disagree, we need to consider the source.

Criteria for Evaluating Online Sources

How do you know which authorities and online sources to trust? When you look for information, you need to know the basis of the author's authority. Here are some questions you can ask to answer the question: How dependable is the source?

- Is the authority well-known and well-regarded?

- What are the authority's credentials (position, institutional affiliation)? You can check the Web page for a biography, check links to other documents, or check the author's homepage.

- Was the authority in a position to have access to pertinent facts? Someone who was a firsthand observer of the events in question is usually (but not always) more reliable. In general, primary sources are more impressive than secondary sources.

- Has the authority been screened by some organization? For example, articles in academic journals are evaluated by peers--experts in the field--to help determine if they should be accepted for publication.

- What are the likely biases? Factors that can influence how evidence is reported are personal needs, prior expectations, general beliefs, attitudes, values, theories, and ideologies. Few experts are without bias, but some have less bias than others. We can try to determine that bias by seeking information about the authority's personal interest in the topic of discussion. We need to be especially wary if an authority stands to benefit financially from the actions he or she advocates.

- How scholarly and fair has the author been? Does the author show knowledge of related sources, with appropriate citations? If claims need empirical support, does the author provide research evidence? If the topic is controversial, does the author acknowledge this and present several sides of the issue, or is the presentation one-sided? Does the document include a full biography, with references to high-quality sources, including primary sources and recent scholarly reviews? Is the information recent and up-to- date?

- Is the information timely and up-to-date? When was it produced and last updated?

Differences Among Sources of Information on the Web

The motives and purposes of those who put up websites vary greatly, and those differences affect the quality of the information. To determine the likely motives of website sponsors, you need to know who the sponsors are. Try to determine the following about any site you are using for information:

- The name of the organization or individual responsible.
- Links to additional information about the organization or individual.
- A clear statement of the site's goals.
- A clear indication of any financial sponsors and whether they are profit or nonprofit.

Your next question is: What are the likely motives of the source? Some possibilities:

- **To inform**. Many websites exist simply to present information on a topic. URL addresses that end in **.edu** or **.gov** tend to be informational because they are sponsored by educational institutions or by government agencies. Some examples: Library of Congress (lcweb.loc.gov), U.S. Environmental Protection Agency (www.epa.gov), the Internet Encyclopedia of Philosophy (www.utm.edu/research/iep/) and the U.S. Department of Commerce (www.commerce.gov).

- **To advocate.** The purpose of an advocacy page is to persuade you. Such pages reflect strong biases, which you need to identify in judging the quality of the information. URL addresses often end in **.org** if they are sponsored by a nonprofit organization. If a site's authors and sponsors seek financial donations, promote a cause, try to recruit members to an organization or provide ways for like-mind people to pursue further contact, it is an advocacy page. Organizations like Planned Parenthood, the National Rifle Association, the National Organization for Women, the Christian Coalition, and the ACLU sponsor advocacy sites.

- **To sell.** The primary purpose of many websites is to promote or sell products or services; you need to be especially alert to biases in information from such sites. URL addresses whose purpose is to sell often end in **.com**. Examples: Amazon.com, Ebay, the Gap, and Circuit City.

- **To provide news.** Many of these sites are postings of news from traditional print sources such as *The New York Times*, *USA Today*, *Newsweek*, and *Time*. Some news sites (Slate.com and Salon.com, for example) gather information from and link to multiple news sites as well as providing their own content.

- **To express individual opinions**. Many websites are created by individuals who want to express themselves. They may take the form of online journals, art galleries, or poetry sites. Web logs, called "blogs," whose authors comment on issues and link to news sites or like-minded Web authors, are increasingly popular. Personal opinion Web pages are very diverse and often very biased. Find out as much as you can about the person behind the site to decide how much credence to give his or her opinions.

- **Mixed motives.** Websites often reflect multiple motives. Be especially alert to sites that suggest one motive (information) but actually reflect other important motives (such as selling). An example is the "teen health" site listed on Yahoo! that is sponsored by a men's magazine--it blankets the site with advertising for health products. Another common practice is to make a website look as though it is informing when it is also advocating. If you are writing a paper on gun control, you may want to review sites sponsored by both pro- and anti-gun groups, but keep in mind their biases before you use any information from them.

Omitted Information

The information that you find at any particular site is selective. There are limitations imposed by time and space. Readers have limited attention spans and the communicator's knowledge is always incomplete. Sometimes, an author means to deceive: advertisers omit information that reflects badly on their products, and experts sometimes leave out information that would weaken their arguments. Finally, people have different values, beliefs, and attitudes. An individual's perspective may prevent him from noting information presented by those with different perspectives.

To get a fair picture of an issue or make a sound judgment on a research question, you need to pursue the omitted information. As you read a document, ask yourself questions to help you fill in what is missing:

- **Counterarguments**. What reasons would someone who disagrees offer? Are there research studies that contradict the studies presented? Are there missing examples that support the other side of the argument?

- **Definitions**. How would the arguments differ if key terms were defined in other ways?

- **Value preferences or perspectives**. From what other set of values might one approach this issue?

- **Origins of "facts" alluded to in the argument**. Are the factual claims supported by well-done research or by reliable sources?

- **Process used for gathering facts**. Was a survey conducted scientifically? How were respondents chosen and how were questions worded?

- **Figures, graphs, and data**. Would statistical results look different if they included evidence from different years? Have figures been selected to make a stronger case?

- **Effects of what is advocated or opposed**. What are the proposal's impacts, positive and negative, short- and long-term? Could there be unintended consequences? Which segments of society would gain and which would lose? What about other impacts: political, economic, biological, spiritual, health, interpersonal, or environmental?

- **Benefits accruing to the author**. Will the author benefit financially if we adopt his or her proposal?

Of course, reasoning is always incomplete. You could never form an opinion if you believed you had to find every possible piece of information on the subject first. But you can improve your arguments and your writing by gathering the most reliable and current information possible, given your limitations of time and space.

Chapter 3

Avoiding Plagiarism and Using Sources Ethically

What Is Plagiarism?

It is plagiarism to present another person's words or ideas as if they were your own. A kind of theft, plagarism can result in failing a course or even in expulsion from college. While blatant, intentional plagiarism is not the campus norm, many students fail to fully understand what constitutes plagiarism. Internet research in particular poses pitfalls: information can be copied from the Web with the click of a mouse, and too many students wrongly believe that anything on the Internet is in the public domain (see the section "Using Copyrighted Materials" at the end of this chapter). Others believe that they can escape detection because a professor couldn't read all the possible sources on a topic; however, instructors can now access websites that scan documents and search the Internet to identify plagiarized material.

The most flagrant forms of plagiarism are the use of another student's work, the purchase of a "canned" research paper, or knowingly copying passages into a research paper without documentation. Sometimes students unintentionally plagiarize through carelessness--by leaving off quotation marks or failing to document sources properly. Also, too many students believe that merely changing sentence order or a few words in a passage avoids plagiarism.

How to Avoid Plagiarism

Always credit the source for any ideas and words not your own. That said, a fear of plagiarism should not force you to document the obvious. You do not have to document common knowledge--information that most educated people know. (For example, that George W. Bush did not win the popular vote in the 2000 presidential election is common knowledge; a newspaper citation would be unnecessary.) You also do not have to document your own thinking, including points or conclusions that you have reached through the course of your research.

Paraphrasing

When you paraphrase, you restate *in your own words* a passage written or spoken by another person--and no more. Your writing should reflect the original passage's emphasis in your own phrasing and sentence structure. Compare the following passages. Here's the original, from a Stanford University website on South Africa:

> With the enactment of apartheid laws in 1948, racial discrimination was institutionalized. Race laws touched every aspect of social life, including a prohibition of marriage between non-whites and whites, and the sanctioning of "white-only" jobs. In 1950, the Population Registration Act required that all South Africans be racially classified into one of three categories, white, black (African) or colored (of mixed descent). The colored category included major subgroups of Indians and Asians. Classification into these categories was based on appearance, social acceptance and descent. For example, a white person was defined as "in appearance obviously a white person or generally accepted as a white person." A person could not be considered white if one of his or her parents were non-white. The determination that a person was "obviously white" would take into account "his habits, education and speech, and deportment and demeanor" (Chokshi, Carter, Gupta, Martin, & Allen, 1991).

Unacceptable Paraphrase (underlined words are plagiarized):

> According to Chokshi et al. (1991), racial discrimination was institutionalized with passage of the apartheid laws in 1948. Race laws touched every aspect of social life, including banning marriage between races, and the sanctioning of "white-only" jobs. The 1950 Population Registration Act required that all South Africans be racially classified as white, black (African) or colored (of mixed descent, Indian or Asian). Classification was based on appearance, social acceptance and descent. A white person, for example, was "in appearance obviously a white person or generally accepted as a white person." A person could not be considered white if one of his parents were non-white. According to the act, determining that a person was "obviously white" would take into account "his habits, education and speech, and deportment and demeanor.

In the above example, citing the authors (Chokshi et al., meaning "Chokshi and others") at the beginning does not legitimize using the authors' exact wording-- nor does changing a few words and the order of phrases.

Acceptable Paraphrase:

> The 1948 apartheid laws made racial discrimination official. The wide-ranging laws allowed "white-only" jobs and banned marriage between races. Two years later, the Population Registration Act classified all South Africans into one of three racial categories: white, black

(African) or colored. "Colored" South Africans were of mixed descent or were Indians or Asians. According to Chokshi et al. (1991), the categories were determined by "appearance, social acceptance and descent." An officially "white" person, then, had been judged to look like a white person or was accepted as one. A white person could not have a non-white parent. The act posited that "habits, education and speech, and deportment and demeanor" would help determine the classification.

Here, the writer has borrowed two phrases from the original, but enclosed them in quotes or attributed them properly--to Chokshi et al. and the Population Registration Act.

Summarizing

A summary condenses the essentials of someone else's thought into a few statements. A summary is shorter than a paraphrase and provides only the main point from the original source. Keep it short; a summary should reduce the original by at least half. As with a paraphrase, keep your own ideas and opinions separate; you may want to note them to yourself and use them elsewhere in your paper, however.

Here is how the above quotation could be summarized:

The 1948 apartheid laws institutionalized racial discrimination in South Africa, affecting all aspects of social life. The 1950 Population Registration Act set up three categories of races, determined by such factors as appearance and descent (Chokshi, Carter, Gupta, Martin & Allen, 1991).

How to Include Reference Citations in Your Text

As you take notes, keep meticulous track of your sources. You may want to print a hard copy of each Web article used in order to save the author or authors, organization, title, date and URL for later reference--especially since Web pages are created and taken down constantly. Find out which documentation standard your instructor is using. The major styles used are MLA (Modern Language Association), APA (American Psychological Association), CMS (Chicago Manual of Style), or CBE (Council of Biology Editors, now the Council of Science Editors). All of these styles may be found on the Research Navigator homepage (www.researchnavigator.com) at the "Citing Your Sources" tab.

Here's how the entry on your "Works Cited" page would look for the apartheid quote using APA style:

Monal Chokshi, Cale Carter, Deepak Gupta, Tove Martin & Robert Allen (1991). Computers and the apartheid regime in South Africa. *South Africa. Guide to Internet Resources. Stanford University.* Retrieved Dec. 12, 2002, from the World Wide Web: http://www-cs-students.stanford.edu/~cale/cs201

In the example above, the authors' names are followed by the year the paper was written, the paper's title, and the name of the website (in italics). The date it was retrieved is followed by the URL. If the source is from a journal, you'll need to include the title of the periodical or electronic text, volume number, and pages.

The process for citing a Web source within text is similar to citing a print source. Within your text, you will need to provide enough information to identify a source with a name or website. If the site includes page numbers or paragraph numbers, use those as well. (In subsequent references to the same authority, the author's last name is usually sufficient.) Keep citations brief; you will fully document each source on the "Works Cited" page. If no author is listed, use the article title or website information for your in-text citation:

> South Africa's minority government used technology--especially computer hardware and software--as a tool of repression (*Computers and the Apartheid Regime in South Africa*, 1991).

Quoting Sources

Direct quotations from online material follow the same rules as non-Internet material. Enclose within quotations marks all quoted materials--a phrase, a sentence, a paragraph. (Some documentation styles specify that if you are quoting more than a sentence or two, the quote should be indented instead and set off typographically.)

Don't load a paper with quotations; if more than a quarter of your essay consists of quotations, you are letting others speak for you and giving the impression that you have not synthesized the material. When drawing from an authority, rely mostly on paraphrase and summary. *Do* use a quotation, however, when it fits your message and its language is particularly on point or if the idea is hard to paraphrase accurately.

> Diane Sollee (1996), the founder and director of the Coalition for Marriage, Family and Couples Education, said, "The number one predictor of divorce is the habitual avoidance of conflict."

Quote exactly; if you drop a quoted phrase within a sentence, make sure the grammar meshes with your own. If you eliminate a sentence or words within the quote, use ellipses according to the appropriate documentation style.

Halberstam (2001) described "… a dramatically changed America, one which has been challenged by the cruelest kind of terrorism, and which is in a kind of suspended state between war and peace …and where so much of our normal agenda has been brushed aside."

Using Copyrighted Materials

Just as a patent protects an inventor's rights to exploit a new product, a copyright signifies original creation and ownership of written words, music, or images. As a student, you may use copyrighted material in your research paper under the doctrine of fair use, which allows the use of others' words for such informational purposes as criticism, comment, news reporting, teaching, scholarship, or research. Academic integrity requires documenting such use in the manner covered in this chapter.

Copyright law is not intended to halt the flow of ideas and facts; it is meant to protect the literary, musical, or visual form that an author or artist uses to express his concepts. For example, there is a popular poem called "Warning" by Jenny Joseph (1961) that begins, "When I am an old woman I shall wear purple/ With a red hat which doesn't go and doesn't suit me." Several websites publish a shorter, adapted version of the poem, but anyone who wants a full version is directed to buy products from a company that has bought publishing rights to the poem. If anyone could sell products displaying Joseph's poem, its value to Joseph and the authorized publisher would be greatly diminished. Few artworks are as commercial as this, but a literary critic who published, without permission, all seven lines of a seven-line poem in her review would be violating copyright law as well. In either case, it *is* permissible to describe the ideas and facts contained in a work or quote brief passages; what is *not* permissible is to copy or reprint large portions of the work in its original literary, musical, or visual format without permission.

If you use substantial blocks of material, or you want to download images for your paper, you should seek permission from the author or website. When in doubt, consult your instructor or e-mail the author or another contact for the Internet site.

Chapter 4

Introducing
Research Navigator™

What Is Research Navigator
and How Can It Help with Research?

Research Navigator is an online academic research service that combines three major databases with practical research assistance--all in one place on the Web. It can help you understand the steps in the research process while also providing in-depth information on conducting library research.

Research Navigator offers these databases of credible and reliable source material: EBSCO's ContentSelect Academic Journal and Abstract Database, The *New York Times* Search by Subject Archive, and "Best of the Web" Link Library. It also guides students step-by-step through the writing of a research paper. Access to Research Navigator is free with the purchase of any Pearson Education college textbook.

To begin using Research Navigator, register with the personal access code found in this *Guide to Online Research*. Once you register, you have access to all the resources in Research Navigator for six months.

What's in Research Navigator?

From the homepage, you can gain access to all of the site's main features, including the three databases--for academic journals and general interest publications (EBSCO's ContentSelect), newspaper articles (The *New York Times* Search by Subject Archive), and World Wide Web sites ("Best of the Web" Link Library)--that will be discussed in greater detail later. If you are new to the research process, you may want to start by browsing "Understanding the Research Process," located in the upper right-hand section of the homepage. Here you will find help on all aspects of conducting research, from gathering data to searching the Internet, evaluating sources, drafting the paper, and revising and editing the final draft.

ContentSelect

EBSCO's ContentSelect Research Database gives you instant access to thousands of academic journals and periodicals from any computer with an Internet connection.

When you need the most authoritative take on a subject, especially one that is complex or very specialized, you will turn to academic journals. Academic journals are aimed at a professional audience--researchers, instructors, and experts, usually affiliated with colleges and universities. Academic-journal articles have been peer-reviewed before publication; that is, they have been checked for balance, methodology, and significance by other experts in the field. An article that doesn't meet the profession's standards will not be published in an academic journal. Examples of academic journals are *Science, Nature, American Ethnologist, Journal of Chemical Education*, and *Canadian Journal of Sociology.*

When you do a search, your list will include some results in full-text format. The full article may be in HTML, the common language used to write Web documents, or it may be in a PDF format. PDF is a file format that creates high-resolution documents; to read such documents, however, you need to first download a free viewer, Adobe Acrobat Reader.

Many ContentSelect results will be in a citation format; when you click on those results, you will get a biblographic reference with author, subject, and journal source. A citation will usually contain an abstract, or brief summary of the article, that will help you determine whether you want to find the full article. You then find the full article through the journal's online archive, or in a print or electronic version through your college library's catalog.

To use ContentSelect, select a database to search and then enter a keyword. For more detailed information, see Chapter 7.

The *New York Times*
Search by Subject Archive

Among daily newspapers, the *New York Times* is the gold standard. It is widely considered the nation's newspaper of record because it is comprehensive and staffed by reporters and editors who are experienced and well-regarded. It has substantial resources and a tradition of excellence.

The *Times*, however, like other newspapers, is aimed at a general audience and is limited by daily deadlines, competitive pressures, and space, so individual articles may not be suitable sources for a complex or very specialized research topic. But for day-to-day coverage of events and popular issues, and general, accessible background information on a wide range of topics, it is first rate.

Research Navigator gives you access to a one-year archive of articles from the *New York Times*. The archives are searchable by subject and by keyword. For tips on how to use the *New York Times* archive, see Chapter 5. Articles can be printed or saved for later use in your research assignment. Be sure to review the rules for citing a newspaper article in endnotes or a bibliography.

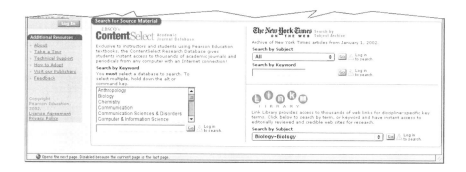

Link Library

Link Library is a collection of links to websites, organized by academic subject and key terms. To use this database, select a subject from the drop-down list. You will be taken to a list of key terms; find the key term for your subject and see a list of five or more editorially reviewed websites that offer educationally relevant and credible content. The Web links in Link Library are monitored and updated each week, reducing your chances of encountering dead links.

Other Resources within Research Navigator

Using Your Library

Despite the Internet revolution, a visit to a bricks-and-mortar library continues to be an important part of the research process. Use the drop-down list on the

Research Navigator homepage "Using Your Library" tab to select a "Library Guide" for your subject. The guide will list Library of Congress and Dewey call numbers, major print and online journals, organizations and associations, discussion lists, and Internet resources. Print it out and take it with you to help you navigate a library's vast resources more efficiently.

"Using Your Library" also discusses types of libraries, their resources, how to choose which ones to use, and the research process and how to develop a timeframe for it.

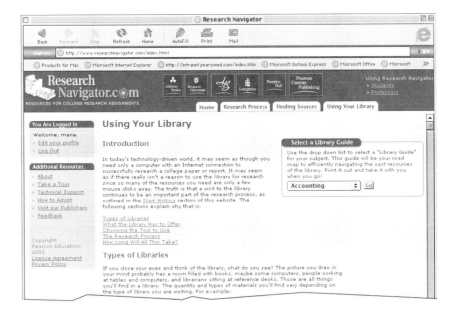

The Research Process

There are several key steps to the research process, beginning with the selection of a research topic and the development of a tentative thesis. The three hyperlinked sections under the "Research Process" tab--"Start Writing," "Internet Research," and "Citing Sources"--explain the research process in greater detail, including how to evaluate good source material, how to properly cite sources, and how to develop endnotes or a bibliography.

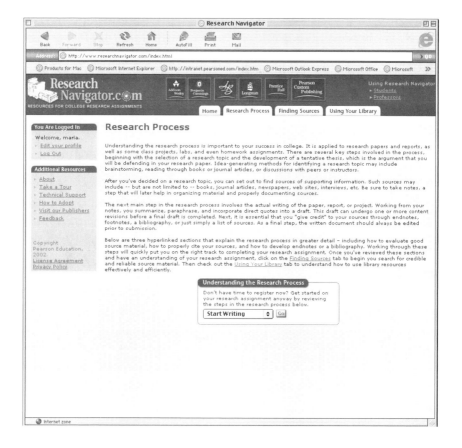

Finding Sources

This section of Research Navigator helps start your search for credible and reliable source material by offering three databases of source material, similar to those offered by a library. EBSCO's Academic Journal and Abstract Database gives you journal articles from leading academic journals as well as articles from many leading popular periodicals, such as *Newsweek* and *USA Today*. The *New York Times* Search by Subject Archive lets you review newspaper articles from the past year, and Link Library points you to the "Best of the Web" sites that have been screened for educational relevance to key topics.

If you need more source material, or are ready to go to the library to conduct a more detailed and thorough search, click on "Using Your Library" and review suggestions for making the most of your time at the library.

Chapter 5

Using the *New York Times* Search by Subject Archive

About the *New York Times*

Newspapers, also known as periodicals because they are issued in periodic installments (e.g. daily, weekly, or monthly), provide contemporary information. Although they don't have the scholarly authority of academic journals, newspapers are often the best source of the latest information on popular and controversial topics. Political struggles, economic debates, election campaigns and issues, scientific advances, the arts and contemporary social trends are all extensively covered by periodicals.

Research Navigator gives you access to a search-by-subject archive of articles from one of the world's leading newspapers: the *New York Times*. Since its founding in 1851, the *New York Times* has become the nation's newspaper of record--the publication that other media look to as a guide for coverage and responsible news judgment. The *Times* is still the leader among news organizations in winning Pulitzer Prizes, journalism's top award, with 108 prizes through 2002. It employs more than 1,000 editors, reporters, photographers, artists, and designers in its news department. Its reach is truly global: in 2001, the *Times* had 30 reporters in Washington, D.C.; 30 reporters in U.S. bureaus outside Washington and New York; and 40 staff correspondents and contributors in 26 news bureaus around the world.

Using the criteria we established in Chapter 2 for the dependability of sources, the *Times*:

- is well-known and well-regarded.
- has impressive credentials (Pulitzer Prizes, experienced reporters and editors).
- has access to pertinent facts (numerous correspondents provide firsthand accounts worldwide).

On the other hand, *Times* content is not peer-reviewed in the way that an academic journal is. Its content *is* screened informally by media observers and critics who are quick to pounce on any perceived errors or biases. In recent years, questions have been raised about the *Times'* coverage of a cancer "breakthrough," an Asian-American scientist suspected of being a spy, and attendance at anti-Iraq-war rallies. When *Times* editors have been convinced that criticisms have merit, they have published follow-up stories or editor's notes acknowledging errors of fact or emphasis. When smaller factual errors come to light, the *Times*, like most leading newspapers, prints timely corrections; some online archives, such as LexisNexis, append the corrections to the story.

So, while the *Times* is an excellent source for information on current topics, keep in mind that it has daily deadlines, competitive pressures, and fallible editors and reporters--like all newspapers. You need to apply the same skepticism toward the information it provides as you would with any other source. Check factual claims with other sources and be alert for signs of bias and omitted information.

What's in the Archive?

Research Navigator's *New York Times* archive organizes articles published in the past year by more than 135 academic subjects, from accounting to zoology. It only includes articles deemed relevant and timely for research; you will not find recipes or wedding announcements. The *Times* archive contents are updated every day.

The *Times'* regular website, www.nytimes.com, contains the full content of the print edition as well as additional articles and images. The newspaper's own archive includes articles from as far back as January 1, 1996, but at the time this guide was written, the *Times* charged a fee to access articles--except for art, book, and entertainment reviews--that were more than seven days old.

When and How to Use *New York Times* Articles

If you want to know the latest on an issue or breaking news story, check Research Navigator's *New York Times* archive. Want to know the status of congressional action regarding offshore income-tax shelters? What are the most recent developments with charter schools? What are the two political parties' stands on affirmative action? Go to the relevant subject directory, or do a keyword search, or both.

But if you are researching existential philosophers, European colonialism in the Congo, or the photography of Walker Evans, for example, a newspaper archive is not the place to start. For non-contemporary subjects, especially complex academic topics, you should consider academic journals, subject directories, and search engines for finding online sources. Research Navigator's ContentSelect and Link Library, which are explained in the next two chapters, will help you find directories and search engines more suited to your topic.

Searching the Archive

Search by Subject

Searching the *New York Times* archive by subject is not only easy, it's also more suited to browsing than to finding a specific topic. The "constitutional law" grouping had 166 articles when this was written, and the "American government" heading had nearly 4,000. But once you have called up a subject area, you are taken to an advanced search page and you can further refine your search with a keyword or words. Articles can be printed or saved for later use. Be sure to review the citation rules for how to cite a newspaper article in endnotes or a bibliography.

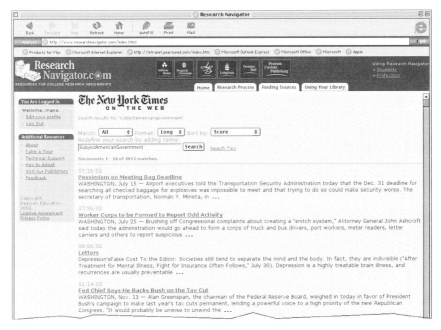

Search by Keyword

Type a word, or multiple words separated by commas, into the search box. If you are using more than one word, there are three **match** options for you to choose from.

- The "All" option will pull up all articles with all of the key terms you enter as well as their various word endings. So, for example, if you search for articles with the words **Enron** and **auditor**, your search results will include articles that contain the words **Enron** and **auditor** as well as articles that contain the words **Enron** and **auditors**.

- The "Any" option is equivalent to the Boolean "or." It will pull up all articles with any of the terms you enter. Using the same key words as above, **Enron** and **auditor**, the "any" option will yield articles that contain the words **Enron** or **auditor** or **auditors**.

- The "Boolean" option lets you use the Boolean operators "and," "or," and "not" to refine your search. See Chapter 2 for more information on using Boolean terms.

In addition, there are two **format** options: "Long" and "Short." The search results for the default, Long, will include headlines and the first five lines from each of the articles. The alternative, Short, will just list the article headlines.

Finally, there are six **sort by** options from which to choose.

- The default, "Score," presents search results in order of the number of times your key words appear in the articles. "Reverse Score" does just the opposite: it lists search results from those articles with the fewest mentions of your key terms first.

- Selecting "Time" will yield results from the most recent to the oldest articles in the archive. Conversely, "Reverse Time" results are presented from oldest to most recent.

- Searching by "Title" will produce articles in alphabetical order based on the first word in the headline. "Reverse Title" will do the opposite.

The most useful of these options are probably the search by "Score," which ranks articles by the number of times they mention your search terms, and "Time" or "Reverse Time," which ranks the articles chronologically.

In the example above, suppose you were researching the role of accounting auditors in the Enron business scandal. At the time this was written, if you used the "Any" option for **Enron** and **auditor**, you'd get 2,708 results, many of them not useful because they included any article from the past year that mentioned "auditor" and any article that included "Enron." If you used the "All" option, you would get 481 results. You could also use the "sort by" options to make the list even more manageable, depending upon whether you wanted the most recent stories (select "Time") or the stories that have more mentions of your terms (select "Score"). If you want to narrow the results yet again, add another keyword. If you searched for **Enron**, **auditor**, and **Andersen** (for the accounting firm), you would get 343 matches. In addition, clicking on the "Long" form will let you read the headline and first paragraph of each article, but using the "Short" form, with headlines only, may help you scan results more quickly.

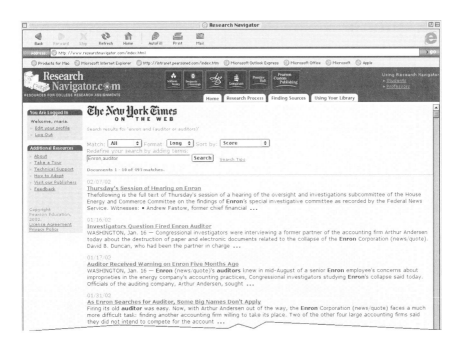

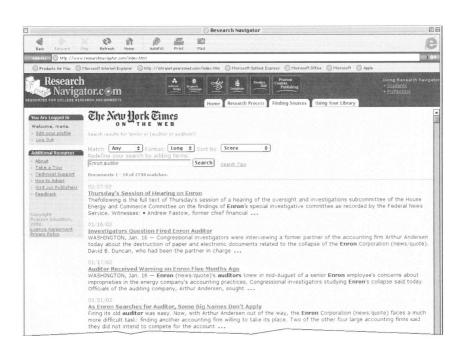

Chapter 6

Using Link Library

Link Library and the Web

Link Library is a collection of Web links, organized into 24 academic subjects, which are in turn divided into subcategories and lists of individual sites. The sites are editorially reviewed, which means that they have been selected because they offer credible and reliable information.

For example, if you were to select the "pollution" subcategory from the **Biology--Environmental Science** subject category, you would get a list of a dozen links. The site topics range from different types of pollution--air, noise, water--to the status of environmental legislation. How dependable are the sources? All are well-known and well-regarded government or educational institutions: the Environmental Protection Agency, NASA Ames Research Center, the University of California at Irvine. Some may quarrel with policies and enforcement efforts of government agencies, but the federal government has a long-established role in collecting data and disseminating information. The government websites listed here cover straightforward, non-controversial subjects: a definition of water pollution, how stratospheric ozone is being depleted, the latest city-by-city air pollution data, etc.

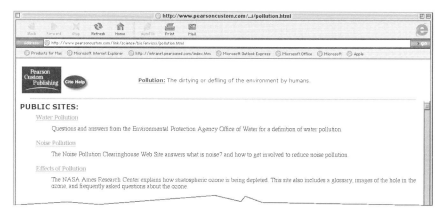

Suppose you look for the same information from websites listed by Yahoo! It turns out that many sites listed under "pollution" are from government and educational agencies. But you will also come across sites like one in which the author describes herself as "devoted to addressing the aspects of the environmental crisis left unacknowledged or inadequately addressed by the vast majority of existing environmental groups." The site is attractive, it doesn't solicit contributions, and it collects articles from generally well-regarded secondary sources, like the Associated Press. But its focus is on opinion, and lists topic headings such as "prophecy" and "prayer." It contains little of scholarly interest and no discernible research evidence. The site's author, while enthusiastic and well-intentioned, is not well-known or well-regarded.

In addition, the Web links in Research Navigator's Link Library are monitored and updated each week to reduce the chance of encountering "dead" links.

What's in Link Library?

Link Library echoes the variety of the World Wide Web. It offers images, text, government and academic documents and research, databases, and search engines. As with any subject directory, you need to narrow your search to the most useful category. You can find links to websites about AIDS, for example, in a half-dozen subject categories: biology, criminal justice, U.S. and world history, philosophy-ethics, and sociology. When you have selected a subject area and found the topic you are seeking, you will find a list of sites. The character of the site you choose to consult will often depend on your topic. The sites in Link Library can be:

- **Scholarly.** If you are researching photosynthesis and you go to the **Biology** subject area, you will find such sites as "What Is Photosynthesis?" and "Photosynthesis Research," maintained by Arizona State University. "Virtual Chloroplast," by the University of Illinois at Urbana-Champaign, contains an image of a chloroplast that lets you click on certain regions for more information.

- **Straightforward.** What if you want information on the 2000 presidential election but don't want to be flooded with opinion pieces about the disputed Florida results? Go to **Political Science – American Government > Presidential Elections**. It has sites such as "Atlas of U.S. Presidential Elections," with voting results for elections dating back to 1860; "U.S. Electoral College," the homepage for the National Archives and Records Administration Guide to the Electoral College; and "Elections," which provides graphs on electoral and popular votes for all U.S. presidential elections to date.

- **Controversial.** You're researching a topic that has heated arguments on both--or many--sides, and you want to summarize the range of public opinion. Link Library subject directories on such topics will lead you to a balanced variety of voices. Under **Philosophy–Ethics**, for example, you will find a list of "partial-birth abortion" links that include a pro-choice site, the text of the *Roe vs. Wade* decision, the National Right to Life Committee homepage, a site that attempts to provide all views of the issue, and a Planned Parenthood site that describes medical procedures performed at various stages of pregnancy.

- **Practical.** Want some help in finding sources on the Web? Go to the **Information Technology** subject directory. The "search engine" heading offers tips for effective Internet searching, common questions about how search engines work, and a chart to help you choose the best search engine for a task.

Finding Information with Link Library

To use this database, you choose a subject from the drop-down list, and, using the alphabetical directory, find the key term for the topic you are searching. Click on the key term and see a list of editorially reviewed websites.

Some topics with wide-ranging aspects appear under more than one subject heading. For example, a list of websites about alcoholism and alcohol abuse can be found under Criminal Justice, U.S. History, General Psychology, and Sociology.

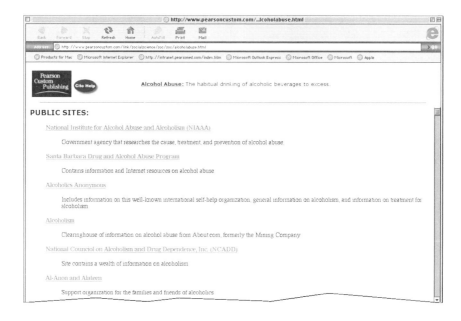

Chapter 7

Using ContentSelect

About ContentSelect

EBSCO's ContentSelect Academic Journal Database is an archive of scholarly peer-reviewed journals and general interest periodicals. Thousands of articles and citations from general interest publications and prestigious academic journals can be instantly accessed in several ways using ContentSelect's search engine. Titles are chosen to reflect multiple perspectives in a range of topics, under 22 broad subject headings in the sciences, humanities, and social sciences.

Of course, ContentSelect is not a substitute for evaluation. Careful research studies sometimes contradict one another, and even authorities disagree. However, while many sources on the Internet may present questionable data or rely on dubious authorities to draw conclusions, ContentSelect provides a wealth of professionally-reviewed information that you can search and evaluate with confidence.

What's in ContentSelect?

ContentSelect offers searchable databases of academic journals and general interest publications. Academic journals are peer-reviewed; general interest publications are not.

Academic Journals
Rather than having a staff of writers who write something on assignment, journals accept submissions from academic researchers all over the country and the world. The journal editor then relies on "peer reviewers," or experts in the author's field, to evaluate the papers submitted to help determine if they should be published. The result is that the content of journal articles meets a higher standard than that of popular magazines, newspaper articles or Web pages. Journals provide specialized knowledge and information about a research topic and adhere to strict professional guidelines for methodology and theoretical grounding.

Scholarly journals are published several times per year. All the issues published in one calendar year constitute a volume. For example, the *American Sociological Review*, the journal of the American Sociological Association, published Volume 65 in the year 2000. That year's volume was made up of six individual issues, numbered Vol. 65 No. 1 and so on.

Additionally, journal issues may contain letters to the editor, book reviews, and comments from authors.

General Interest Publications

In addition to scholarly journals, subject databases--particularly the General Interest database--in ContentSelect include periodicals that are not peer reviewed. Some examples are *Commentary*, *Washington Monthly*, *Newsweek*, *USA Today Magazine*, and the *Christian Science Monitor*. These publications are included because they have articles that are generally credible and reliable. If your topic is timely or controversial, general interest publications may offer more appropriate coverage than academic journals.

Sometimes it's not easy to know at first glance which category a publication fits. For example, you find an article in *Science News*. Is that an academic journal, as the journal *Science* is? When you go to your subject database, click on the "publications" tab. You can scroll down to *Science News* or use the "browse" button to find it. When you click on *Science News*, you'll get an information box that describes the subjects it covers plus a characterization of its content: "presents articles of interest to scientists and others ..." The "and others" is a clue; then, when you check the "peer reviewed" section, it has an "N" for "no." So *Science News* is a general interest publication, not an academic journal. Still, any article in *Science News* is probably reliable, subject to the evaluation you conduct for all sources (see Chapter 2).

Searching ContentSelect

Select a Database

ContentSelect's homepage features a list of databases. To search within a single database, click the name of the database. To search in more than one database, hold down the alt or command key while clicking on the name of the database.

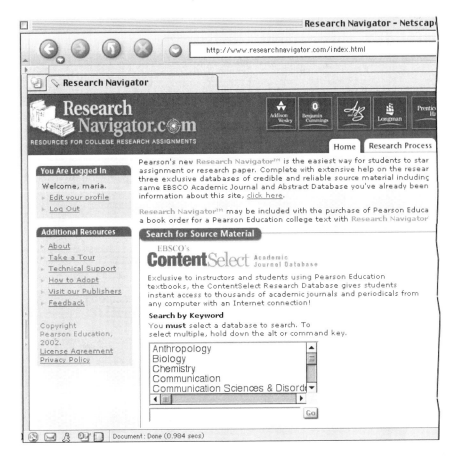

Basic Search

After selecting one or more databases, you must enter a keyword or keywords, then click on "go." This will take you to the basic search window. If you've selected a precise and distinctive keyword, your search may be done. But if you have too many results--which is often the case--you need to narrow your search.

The basic search window lets you create a search using a variety of search methods. Enter your search terms in the **Find** field and select from the available search modes: **standard**, **all words**, **any words**, or **exact phrase**.

Standard Search (Boolean)

- **And** combines search terms so that each result contains all of the terms. For example, search **SUV and conservation** to find only articles that contain both terms.

- **Or** combines search terms so that each result contains at least one of the terms. For example, search **SUV or conservation** to find results that contain either term.

- **Not** excludes terms so that each result does not contain the term that follows the "not" operator. For example, search **SUV not conservation** to find results that contain the term **SUV** but not the term **conservation.**

Using the above examples, suppose you were writing a paper about sport utility vehicles and energy conservation, in light of growing criticism of their low gasoline mileage. If you selected the "General Interest" database from ContentSelect and used the Boolean "or," at the time this was written, you would get 800 results for **SUV or conservation**. If you used the Boolean "and" option, (**SUV and conservation**) you would get only two results:

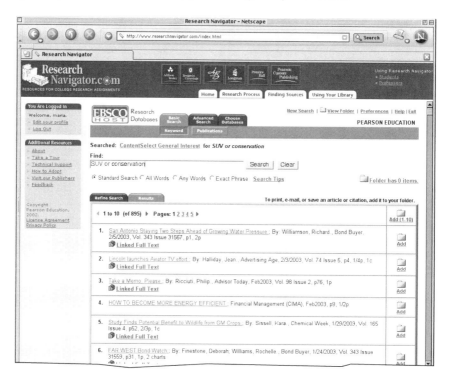

But suppose you decided to write about SUVs and didn't want articles that mentioned the energy conservation issue. If you searched for **SUV not conservation**, you would get 197 results:

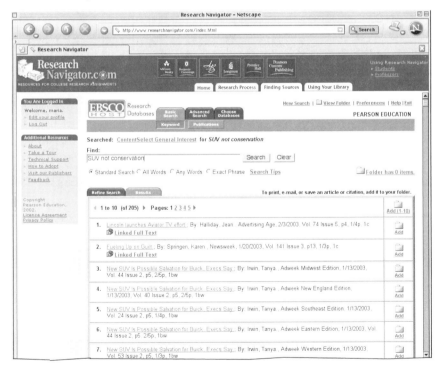

Using "All Words"

In the "All Words" mode, ContentSelect conducts a Boolean search, assuming an AND between each word. The order of the search words entered does not matter. Any results that are displayed must include all words entered, regardless of how close they are to each other. Your search results are presented in order by date.

Using "Any Words"

"Any words" will return pages that include at least one of your terms-- equivalent to using the Boolean "or." For example, if you type in **SUV energy conservation**, you will get results that include one, two, or all three terms.

The more keywords that appear in an article, the more relevant the record is and the closer to the top of the results list it appears. What this means is that you can also enter a phrase or sentence that describes what you want to search for. Any results will appear in ranked order, with the most relevant article presented first.

For example, type **improving gas mileage for SUVs** to find articles that contain **improving, gas, mileage,** or **SUVs**. Prepositions such as **for** and articles such as **the** are excluded from the search. Results at the top of the list will have more (or all) of your keywords than results farther down the list.

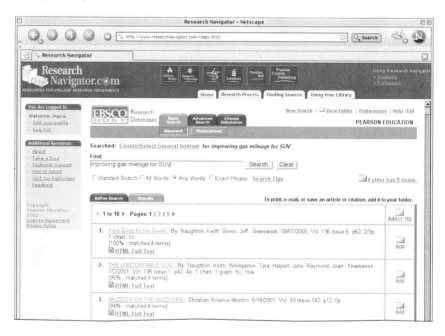

Using "Exact Phrase"

Enter the word or phrase that you want to find. Any results that are displayed will include all the words you entered, exactly as you entered them. (However, stop words--articles and prepositions--are still ignored.) Your search results are presented in order by date.

You can achieve the same results, clicking on any search method, by placing **quotation marks** around search terms. For example, type in **"gas mileage"** and click the "any words" option and you will get the same results you would by typing **gas mileage** and clicking the "exact phrase" option.

Advanced Search

On the tabbed tool bar, click **Advanced Search**. The advanced search window appears. Enter your search terms in the **Find** field. Your search terms can be keywords or selections from search history. Boolean operators (AND, OR, NOT) can also be included in your search.

You can also use **field codes** with your search terms. Fields refer to searchable aspects of an article or Web page; in the case of ContentSelect, they include author, title, subject, abstract, and journal name. Click **Field Codes** to display a list of field codes available with the databases you are using. Type the field code before your search terms to limit those words to the field you entered. For example, **AU Naughton** will find records that contain Naughton in the author field.

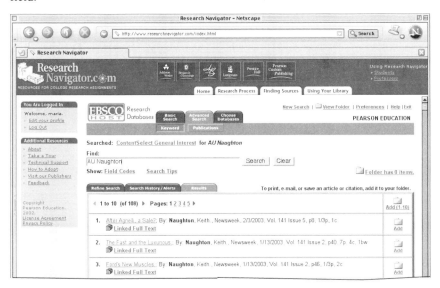

To **print, e-mail, or save** several search results, click on the folder next to the result; then print, e-mail, or save from the folder at the top of the results field. (You can still print, e-mail, or save individual results from the open article or citation.)

You can remove specific results, or clear the entire folder and collect new results, during your session. If you end your session, or it times out due to inactivity, the folder is automatically cleared.

47

Full Text Results

Some ContentSelect results will be available in full text--that is, if you click on the full text logo at the bottom of an entry, you will be able to call up the entire journal or magazine article. If you want to limit your search to results available in full text, click on the "search options" tab, and then on "full text." Then renew your search.

Abstract and Citation Results

Many ContentSelect results are in the form of citations containing abstracts. A **citation** is a bibliographic reference to an article or document, with basic information such as ISSN (International Standard Serial Number, the standard method for identifying publications) and publisher that will help you locate it. An **abstract** is a brief description of an article, usually written by the author. An abstract will help you decide whether you want to locate the work--either in an electronic database or a print version--through your college library.

A handy tip: once you have found an article that meets your research needs, you can search fields easily from the article citation to turn up similar articles. For example, suppose the *Christian Science Monitor* article "Gas-guzzling SUVs muster up a makeover" (Evarts, July 6, 2000) suits your paper perfectly. Go to the citation and click on the subject field to find similar articles. Or, if you want to see what else the author has written, click on the author field to produce a list of articles he has written.

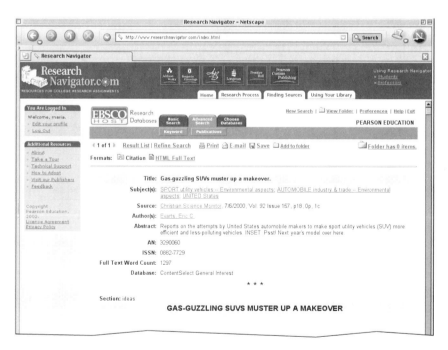

In many cases you can search the full text of articles using electronic databases and then read the entire article online. Typically, in order to use these databases you need to have a library card number or special password provided by the library. But sometimes when you use an electronic database you will find that the text of an article won't be accessible online, so you'll have to go to the library's shelves to find the magazine or newspaper in which the article originally appeared.

For more information, explore "Understanding the Research Process" and "Using Your Library" on the Research Navigator homepage.

Chapter 8

Using Research Navigator and the World Wide Web in Criminal Justice

Introduction

Research Navigator brings the extraordinary power of the Internet and computer technology to your fingertips in a way that is historically unprecedented. Only a decade ago, for example, editorial staff at *Newsweek Magazine* and other national publications dutifully took scissors to each edition of the *New York Times* as well as other leading publications. At *Newsweek*, staffers and interns cut, folded, and filed each *Times* news story under a single subject area. A long row of filing cabinets stuffed with clippings in the *Newsweek* offices one block from the White House was an important resource for some of the most influential political writers in the country.

Then in the early 90's, Lexis-Nexis came along with a service that changed how most people conducted serious research. The company expanded beyond its legal research services and began offering electronic libraries of leading publications (at premium prices), targeting the service to professional researchers, scholars, policy analysts, and mass media institutions, like *Newsweek*. Research tasks that once took several hours could suddenly be completed in just a few minutes.

Lexis/Nexis still boasts 1.5 million subscribers but now many of the services offered ten years ago by the company (and more) are offered at little or very little cost on the Internet. Today, through Research Navigator, you have near instantaneous access to every article in the *New York Times* going back one full year.

Research Navigator and other online tools are redefining college and professional level research, comprehension, and informed decision making. The convenience of Research Navigator and other online tools does not mean that college students and others will spend less time on research anymore than the invention of the automobile meant people spent less time traveling. Properly done, the speed of Internet research translates not only into more information but also better information, making research more interesting, important, and worthwhile.

50

These tools are helping to enhance the educational experience and establishing new benchmarks of scholarship and mastery of subject areas for college students, educators, and all professionals.

This change is no less true in the field of criminal justice, where the responsibility of quickly gathering, analyzing, presenting, and applying new information is as demanding as in any other professional discipline.

Research Navigator is a great tool for projects both big and small. Anyone with a passing familiarity with the Internet will be able to see Research Navigator's utility in writing term papers or other long-term research projects. Research Navigator includes an excellent guide to writing term papers, which can be accessed from the Research Navigator homepage.

In addition, Research Navigator can serve as a companion guide to any criminal justice course. It can help illuminate and clarify events and ideas, confirm information, key players, institutions, or theories. It can aid in finding concrete examples that underscore, or undermine, a controversial theory, or flesh out an abstract idea. It can help establish a timeline of events, and reinforce key concepts. Moreover, by using Research Navigator and other Internet resources as a regular part of your educational endeavors, you will gain experience and proficiency so that you will be better able to use these online tools for whatever educational or professional challenges lie ahead.

To that end, this step-by-step guide demonstrates a few of the many ways that Research Navigator can assist you in the daily challenges of academic and professional pursuits in the criminal justice field, and helps you better familiarize yourself with all that Research Navigator has to offer.

Review of Online Search Strategies

Introduction

The following information is fairly universal, but we will use the *New York Times* search engine on Research Navigator as a specific example to better familiarize yourself with both Internet searching in general and this excellent search device in particular.

There are some basic ideas to keep in mind when performing online searches. These principles apply to Research Navigator as well other search utilities.

One important principle to be mindful of is your purpose for conducting a search. Which Research Navigator tool you select, the kind of key terms you input, and other options you select with respect to searching will depend on what your purpose is in searching. There are three basic types of searches: browsing, locating a specific piece of information, and locating numerous resources on a particular subject.

Browsing

You make browsing searches when you have a broad or open-ended purpose, or you are not exactly sure what you are looking for. You might be looking for ideas or inspiration, or hoping that your initial browsing search will inform subsequent searches.

Examples would be looking for topic ideas for a term paper, searching for information on cities in the Southwestern United States that are good places to live and work, or finding general information on careers in forensic science.

Locating a Specific Piece of Information

This kind of search is like an encyclopedia or dictionary lookup. For example: You want to know the name of the U.S. Attorney General, a brief definition of the exclusionary rule, or what the abbreviation "DNA" stands for. Once you have retrieved this specific information, you have completed the task.

Locating Numerous Resources on a Particular Subject

The third type of search is finding numerous sources on a particular subject so that you can evaluate them and pick those that best suit your purpose. *Trends in federal spending on public safety, Supreme Court decisions relating to the exclusionary rule,* and *the role of DNA in criminal investigations*, are examples of more abstract topics that warrant an evaluation of numerous resources.

Results: Quality, Quantity, and Efficiency

The key in doing research on Research Navigator is narrowing your search so that you find materials that are suitable to your purpose. Two criteria for evaluating the success of your search are:

Precision. Precision is the percentage of document related to your query. For example, fewer than half of the results of a search of the *New York Times* with the word "eagle" or "eagles" will be about the bird that is our national symbol. Some will refer to articles about the United States, such as **'The Eagle's Shadow': Global Village Idiots,** an article about how people abroad, informed by American television, view life in the United States. Most will be about the Philadelphia Eagles football team. So if you are looking for information about large predatory birds, "eagle" is an imprecise search, though it might be adequate in some cases. Even adding the word "bald" does not eliminate all references to the football team. An article by Jere Longman from December 2002 informed readers that "the [Eagles] defense has covered all the bald spots in the offense like a toupee."

Recall. Recall refers to the proportion of relevant documents retrieved out of all possible helpful documents. Adding the word "bald" eliminates most of the articles about the Philadelphia Eagles football team, which is fine if you are doing research on bald eagles. But if you are doing research on all eagles, you have also just eliminated articles about the golden eagle and the crested eagle.

By adding the term "bald" to your search you have improved the precision of your search in that a higher percentage of your returns are relevant to your research, but you have also excluded some materials that might prove valuable.

Nearly all searches involve some tradeoffs: If your search terms are "too general," the search engine will retrieve irrelevant material. Making your query overly specific, however, excludes some of the materials most suitable for your purpose. Ideally, you query the search engine in such a way that you get few if any irrelevant results, without inadvertently excluding any. This Activity Guide explains and illustrates some of the strategies for efficiently retrieving quality information. But before going further into search engine strategies, here are some advanced browser commands that will make your searching go much faster.

Activity: Advanced Navigation Commands
A. Viewing Multiple Pages From Your Desktop
1. Open up your browser to Research Navigator.
2. Open another browser window with the same or even a different browser.
3. Open a Word document.
4. Press [Ctrl + Tab].

What happens?

B. Navigating Within a Web Page
1. Enter the proper name "Ashcroft" in the *New York Times* search engine from the Research Navigator homepage.
2. Click on the headline link of the first article.
3. After Research Navigator retrieves the article, Press [Ctrl + F].
4. Another search box will appear.
5. Enter "Ashcroft" into this search box.
6. Press [Enter].
7. Repeat several times.
8. What happens when you do this?
9. Now press [Ctrl + Home].

What happens?

Answer: You should return to the top of the article.

Changing Your Homepage
When doing online research you can save a lot of time if you make your primary research tool your personal homepage, even if only temporarily. Your personal homepage is the Web page that displays when you first open your browser. Pressing [Alt + Home] will return you to the homepage in your browser. If you know you are going to return frequently to a page, [Alt + Home] is a convenient alternative to the "Back" button or retyping in the URL of the page you are frequenting. With Internet Explorer you can change your homepage by selecting: "Tools," at the top of the browser, and then selecting "Internet Options." Research Navigator does have a convenient "Home" tab in the top center of every page. But familiarizing yourself with some of these search strategies can save valuable time in the long run.

Locating Information with Research Navigator's *New York Times* Archive

In a 1999 article on the nation's best newspapers, the *Columbia Journalism Review* ranked the *New York Times* the #1 newspaper in the country.

Head and shoulders above everyone else, according to the CJR, and "still the nation's newspaper of record." The *Times'* strong local coverage includes not just the city itself but surrounding communities, which range from inner city neighborhoods, to affluent suburbs, to communities not very different from the small rural communities of Ohio or Illinois. The newspaper's international coverage is strong and influential, and its coverage of national politics is second only to the *Washington Post* in terms of its national influence.

The *New York Times* Archive is an incredibly useful tool for conducting research in criminal justice or in any area. It is a great starting point for researching the events, issues, and ideas that shape our world.

The *New York Times* Archive Search Utility

After you log in, you can access the *New York Times* (NYT) Archive directly from the Research Navigator homepage under the *Times* logo.

The top Search window is called "Search by Subject." There are about 140 subjects in all. Try doing a search on the subjects "Criminal Law" and "Law" without adding a keyword.

After you do a search, the "Results Page" lists the articles your query retrieved, along with Title links to stories and the first sentence or two from each article.

Activity
A. Perform a Subject search on "Criminal Law" and "Law."
How many articles did the subject search "Criminal Law" retrieve?
How many articles did the subject search "Law" retrieve?
B. Perform the same two searches, only this time add the word "crime" to your search. Press the word "go" next to the *top* search window.
How many articles did the search engine retrieve under "Criminal Law" with the key word "crime"? How many articles did the search engine retrieve under "Law" with this keyword? Was there a difference? The answer should be no. These two search engines work completely independently of one another. Entering a word or phrase into the keyword box does not alter the results. This is an example of how the number of "results" can serve as a useful gauge for checking your understanding of the how the search utility functions.

Scanning the Subject Areas
Scanning the subject areas is a helpful form of browsing. It demonstrates just

how broad the coverage of the *New York Times* is. Everyone has a tendency to look up topics in familiar ways; the subject guide helps you look at familiar topics in new ways.

Activity

A. Besides the obvious subjects, Criminology, Criminal Law, and Law, what are some of the other categories in the Search By Subject search that might be useful for a criminal justice research project on racial profiling?

Scanning By Subject AND Keyword

If you do an initial search on African American Studies, in addition to search results for this general search of a broad topic, the search box automatically contains the following:

[SubjectAfricianAmericanStudies]

You can now add the search term "racial profiling" to your search and look for racial profiling articles within this particular subject area.

[SubjectAfricianAmericanStudies racial profiling]

The Search by Subject search engine is helpful for inputting the right syntax, but you can input this search manually, too.

Activity

A. How many articles are retrieved for the following three searches from the results page?

[SubjectAfricianAmericanStudies racial profiling]
[SubjectCriminology racial profiling]
[SubjectLaw racial profiling]

By checking the quantity of results and scanning the headlines and opening sentences, you can see that the results are different for these different searches.

Options and "Default Settings"

The *NYT* Archive search utility, like most computer software these days, is configured to work in a predetermined way. But it also allows users to tailor these settings to their own needs. The configuration that you encounter before you make any adjustments is referred to in computer parlance as the "default setting."

If you do a keyword search on "racial profiling" from the Research Navigator homepage you get thousands of results. Suppose you decide to narrow your search by adding the term "drivers" to the Search Engine on the Research Navigator results page. You enter:

[racial profiling drivers]

You now have triple the number of articles originally retrieved. You will not have narrowed your search as might be expected, you have actually expanded it.

The reason is that from the Research Navigator homepage, the keyword search engine automatically searches for articles that include *All* the terms entered. So it looks for articles with both the words racial and profiling.

The default setting for the keyword search engine on the results page is different. It automatically searches for *any* of the three words. So it retrieved articles that included the words racial and profiling and drivers.

You can adjust your query to search out either *Any* or *All* terms using the Option Tab called "Match" that appears above the search engine on the results page.

There is also a third option using "Match" called Boolean.

The link next to the search engine on the results page called "Search Tips" explains: "The 'Boolean' option requires that you use 'operators.' These operators ('and,' 'or,' and 'not' are the most common) give you another way to tell the tool how you want your search to work."

Actually, Any and All options are identical to Boolean commands. Searching for [meth labs Midwest] with "Any" is really the same as doing the Boolean search [meth OR labs OR Midwest], while searching meth labs Midwest with "All" is the same as [meth AND labs AND Midwest]. Boolean operators, however, allow you to refine your search even more. You can combine AND with OR: [Meth OR Methamphetamine AND Midwest].

Activity
A. How many documents are retrieved from the query, meth methamphetamine Midwest, with the All option?
How many documents are retrieved from the query, meth methamphetamine Midwest, with the Any option?
How many documents are retrieved from the query, meth OR methamphetamine AND Midwest?
One especially helpful Boolean command is the "NOT" command. **[Eagles NOT football]** is a search that illustrates this point.
B. Suppose you wanted to find information on gang activity in New York City.
How many documents are retrieved from the search **[gangs New York]** with the "All" option?
How many documents are retrieved from **[gangs AND New AND York NOT movie]** with the Boolean option?
How many documents are retrieved from **[gangs AND New AND York NOT movie NOT Mafia]** with the Boolean option?
Note: When using the Boolean option you must put one of the Boolean "operators" (AND, OR, NOT) between all term words. If your Boolean search includes New York it must be entered New AND York. San Diego is San AND Diego. Thank you would be Thank AND You.

Format

The second option tab above the results page search engine is called "Format." There are two options: Long and Short.

Long is the default option and is most helpful for a specific search for information that may not be central the story's overall theme and thus, may not be found in the headline. The Long option provides not only the headline but the first 30 or 40 words to help you get a better idea about what the article is about.

Suppose you wanted to see how New York City Police Commissioner Raymond W. Kelly is managing under the current city budget crisis. You could do an "All" search of [**Raymond W. Kelly**] then look at the headlines and the opening sentences to determine if the articles will be helpful.

If you wanted to know specifically what Raymond W. Kelly's official statements and stated intentions are in response to the city's budget crisis and its impact on law enforcement, you could select the Short Option and do an "All" search on [**Raymond W. Kelly budget crisis**]. You are looking for stories where Kelly's response to the budget crisis is central enough to warrant a mention in the headline. With the short option you can quickly scan the headlines for suitable articles.

Sort By

The third option tab for the *New York Times* Archive search is the "Sort By" option. This option determines in what order news articles are retrieved in the archive. The default setting for "Sort By" is "Score." Score counts the number of times your keyword(s) appear in the article and lists the articles with the most mentions first.

Activity

A. Perform a search on the surname: Bratton

How many mentions of the name "Bratton" appear in the first article retrieved?
How many mentions of the name "Bratton" appear in the tenth article retrieved?
How many mentions of the name "Bratton" appear in the last article retrieved?
Reminder: You can perform a search within an article of a word or phrase by using [Ctrl F].

There are six options from which to choose in what order the *Times* Archive search engine displays your results. The default, Score, presents search results in the order of the number of times your keywords appear in the articles. Reverse Score does just the opposite: It lists search results from those articles with the fewest mentions of your key terms first. You can always adjust the order that you view the search results with the numbers that appear below the search results. The numeral "1" links to Documents 1-10, the "2" links to documents 11-20, etc.

The "Time" option can be helpful for staying current on news in a particular subject area. The search engine with this option retrieves articles from most current to least current.

Activity
A. Perform the following searches using the "Time" and "All" options:

> Criminal Justice research
> Criminal Justice database
> Justice Department
> Domestic Violence
> Identity Fraud

Do you think it would be better to use the "Long Option," or the "Short Option" in keeping up with criminal justice trends in this way?

The "Reverse Time" option can be useful for getting a complete view of a current event, if you missed the initial press coverage, or if an ongoing story takes a new turn that makes it interesting for you. Perhaps a story about new legislation only made national headlines while it was being voted on and you are now interested in more than a quick review of what led up to the legislation.

Activity
A. Perform a search on the "Department of Homeland Security" using the "All," "Short," and "Reverse Time" Options.
What is the earliest relevant story you can find?

The "Title" option of the archive search engine retrieves articles in alphabetical order by the headline. The alphabetical order of the headline rarely has any relevance to a search, but it might be helpful in randomizing the results with respect to the "Time" and "Score" options, if you have been frustrated by your previous search attempts.

Saving What You Find
In terms of saving your results, the Research Navigator has a strength in this area, as well as a weakness that can be overcome. You should already know how to copy and paste information from an article and how to add "Favorites" to your Web browser.

The Research Navigator site uses a Web design technology called "frames." Thanks to frames, when you visit a particular *New York Times* article and enter [Ctrl +A], you highlight the entire article. You can then easily copy and paste the article into another document. This is a task that is usually difficult to execute on a typical newspaper Web page. Without frames, you would have to manually highlight the articles and might still end up copying parts or all of the surrounding Research Navigator information.

The downside of frames with Research Navigator is that since the specific address information shown at the top of the browser does not provide a path to the article, you cannot quickly add the article to your "Favorites" and revisit the article later.

However, if you highlight and copy the headline from the results page (i.e. **Ashcroft's Terrorism Policies Dismay Some Conservatives**) you can paste the link into a Word document. The link will work as long as you are already logged onto the Research Navigator. Once you access the link from a Word document, your browser will show the link's complete path and you can then add it to your Favorites.

Anatomy of a Search Using the *New York Times* Archive

I wanted to confirm information about the law enforcement official who made national headlines for his role in the investigation and eventual capture of the "Beltway Sniper." I remember he was involved in county government somehow. While most county law enforcement agencies have sheriffs, the county I had in mind had the title "Chief." I started my search by entering some terms right from the search engine box on the Research Navigator homepage:
   [Beltway Sniper]
 I could have entered in a subject at this point too, but "Beltway Sniper" might be specific enough to get the desired result.

When I conducted this search on February 25, 2003, Research Navigator brought me to a new Web page containing the following results:

Documents 1 - 10 of 770 matches.

10/23/02
Bus Driver Killed; Sniper's Threat to Children Revealed
SILVER SPRING, Md., Oct. 22 — A bus driver quietly pausing before his morning rounds was shot to death near here today, leaving alarmed residents and the police fearing that the man was the 10th fatality attributable to the roving suburban sniper. The police also said the attacker warned three days
. . .
10/27/02
In the Sights of the Sniper: 23 Fearful Days in October
WASHINGTON, Oct. 26 — With a loud crack and a blinding light of the SWAT team's disorienting but harmless "flash bang," the agents rushed the blue Chevrolet Caprice parked in a highway rest stop in rural Maryland. They smashed out several windows and unlocked the doors. Within seconds, the ...

10/13/02

Wary, Defiant Suburbanites Carry On in Sniper's Shadow

WASHINGTON, Oct. 12 — As the sun peeped out over the rain-slicked pavement today, people across this sniper-wary region found themselves unwittingly hopscotching through a series of mental calculations in going on about their day. Venture out, but do not dawdle. Run errands, but watch for white vans ...

10/11/02

Police Confirm Sniper's Link to 7th Killing

MANASSAS, Va., Oct. 10 — The sniper had already moved on hours earlier in the rain by the time ballistic experts finally confirmed his seventh killing in eight days. Washington area residents were already deeper into their fears, waiting for his next move. "It's a whodunit at this point," ...

10/12/02

Accommodating Fears in a Sniper's Killing Field

TYSONS CORNER, Va., Oct. 11 — Ashley Neece called her boyfriend as she drove to get gas on Leesburg Pike near the entrance to the Beltway today. She hung up the phone to pump, then called him again as soon as she was done. "He said to call him and let him know I was O.K.," she said. At a ...

10/22/02

Richmond Is Jolted by a Sniper's Attack and Its Aftermath as Well

RICHMOND, Va., Oct. 21 — They unleashed the Blackhawk helicopter, the SWAT team, scores of federal agents and even a spy plane. But by day's end, the big sting that the authorities said went down in the suburbs of Richmond, with two men collared in a white minivan, appeared to be worth as much as ...

10/19/02

Students Fidget Through Sniper's Lockdown

CHEVY CHASE, Md., Oct. 18 — Allie Christman is itchy, itchier by the day. It was mean enough, she said, that her fifth birthday last Sunday had to be hemmed in and rained on by all this bad-guy stuff: The grownups said no outdoor party, no way. But this endless Code Blue situation at school is becoming ...

10/11/02

Experts Debate the Sniper's Links to Popular Culture

SILVER SPRING, Md., Oct. 10 — A frustrating lack of clues in the sniper shootings has prompted speculation about links to popular thrillers, the language of video game enthusiasts and, of course, decks of tarot cards, in particular, the death card, which was found near a school where a 13-year-old ...

10/09/02

Where the Longest Shadow of Autumn Is a Sniper's

SILVER SPRING, Md., Oct. 8 — For seven strange days, each more jittery than the last, a macabre lottery has been playing in Washington and its well-groomed suburbs. It affords everyone who dares leave the house a chance — an infinitesimal chance, but a chance — of being murdered by an excellent marksman ...

10/07/02

Fear in a Sniper's Wake: 'This Guy's Our Neighbor'

ASPEN HILL, Md., Oct. 6 — The police chief, his offerings of fresh information running thin, could offer only a guess today that the elusive dead-aim sniper "may be gloating" nearby in a suburban enclave much like this one. Kevin Boink, a local resident bucking the mood of fear by going shopping ...

None of the first ten results yielded the name I was looking for. At least the name did not appear in the headline or in the first couple of sentences displayed. I had a few options:

1. I could look at the next ten results. This was the least desirable option. Generally, the quality of results drops off quickly. Better to learn how to work with the search engine to deliver quality results from the start.

2. I could go back and specify "Criminology" or "Criminal Law" in the subject area box. In this particular case, the answer wasn't to specify a subject. The results were all on the topic I had in mind. In fact, when I went back and redid the search with the term "sniper," I retrieved exactly the same first ten results.

Entering just "beltway," a nickname for the Washington D.C. metropolitan area, yielded a variety of results but still, half (five out of ten) are still on topic. When I enter "beltway" and specify the subject area "Criminology"

[SubjectCriminology sniper]

from the homepage, I'm back to 100% results.

3. I could look at the first forty words or so of the articles that were displayed along with my search and see if any are likely to contain the name of the official. There are a couple of articles that look like strong candidates for the information I want, but I wanted to see if could find it without scanning articles.

4. I could search again with other key terms.

I decide to make the search more specific by adding an additional word. This time I input into the search engine:

[beltway sniper chief]

The first results yielded the name of Montgomery County Police Chief Charles A. Moose in the opening sentence visible to me without going to the article.

61

It's a story from early on in the investigation. It reports that Moose played a central role at the outset. But did he play a pivotal role in the capture of the two suspects? I was pretty sure he was the individual I was looking for information on, but I decided to keep with my search to confirm it.

The search engine results page allows a visitor to adjust the parameters of a search beyond topic area and key word. The first one is called "Match." The initial search from the Research Navigator home page was preset for "Any" in the "Match" box, which has three options in all. A preset parameter in computer parlance is often referred to as the "default" setting. For my search of "beltway sniper chief," the search engine retrieved articles in which any of these terms appeared. I decided to adjust the Match setting so that instead of finding articles with any of the terms, it would retrieve articles with *all* of the terms. I again do the search:

[beltway sniper chief]

My search returned only three results, and none mentioned Chief Charles A. Moose by name in the beginning of the article. The headlines looked promising though, so I made a mental note to redo this search and check these articles if I couldn't find what I was looking for with another search strategy.

I then try to answer the question: "Were there any other chiefs besides Chief Moose who played a leading role in the investigation? I next try the Boolean Option under Match. With the Boolean Option, all terms must be separated by one of the following words:

1. AND
2. OR
3. NOT

The term "AND" denotes both words. [sniper AND chief] will retrieve articles with both sniper and chief. The term "OR" denotes either word. [sniper OR chief] will retrieve articles with either sniper or chief. The term "NOT" excludes a word. [sniper NOT moose] will retrieve only articles that have the word sniper but not the word (or surname) "moose."

I decided to exclude Moose from my search for articles about the Beltway Sniper by entering:

[beltway AND sniper NOT moose]

None of the initial results return the name of any Chief involved with Beltway Sniper investigation.

The format option offers a choice between the "Long" format and the "Short" format. The Long format is the preset configuration of the search engine. However, you can opt for the Short option which only displays headlines. The "Short Option" can be helpful but didn't really serve my purpose. The third Option, "Sort by" has the default option "Score." The default, Score, presents search results in order of the number of times your key words appear in the article. This seemed like the best choice for my purpose.

I decided to go back and redo the search "beltway sniper chief" and select the "All" option under "Match."

One of the articles included the following: "But administration says...that Mr. Bush has been deliberately circumspect in his remarks for fear of disturbing the continuing communications between the sniper and Chief Moose." I was now convinced I had the right individual. But on a lark I entered:
[moose]
The first article listed appears to be a profile of Chief Charles A. Moose. The headline is:
The Challenge of a Career Ends With Success for Moose

Despite my somewhat circuitous strategy, I did manage to locate the person I was interested in finding out about, confirmed that it was the right person, and familiarized myself with the topic through numerous newspaper accounts addressing a variety of facets of the case.

Researching with EBSCO's ContentSelect

The EBSCO ContentSelect™ collection of resources is culled from thousands of academic articles, organized by discipline. Articles from periodicals such as *Newsweek* and the *Christian Science Monitor* are included as well, providing access to topical content from an amazing variety of sources.

You can start searching ContentSelect right from the Research Navigator homepage. ContentSelect is an exponentially larger database than the *New York Times*. It includes research reports from scholars and scientists that sometimes serve as the basis for news stories in the *New York Times* and other newspapers. With ContentSelect you can search subject databases about a particular topic, or search topics by publication or author or both at once!

Searching with ContentSelect
Using ContentSelect is a little bit more complicated at first than a search engine like Google, but it is well worth the effort given the quality of the resources in this database.

Keyword *and* Database Search. Unlike the *New York Times* Archive search engine, the "Keyword" search window and the "Database" (Subject) window on the Research Navigator homepage work in tandem. In fact, you are *required to* select both a Database and enter a keyword to begin a search. After you have made a keyword search, with one or more of the selected databases you can refine your search parameters from the results page.

Keyword Search Options. ContentSelect recognizes four options for keyword searching:

Standard Word Search: Recognizes and requires one of the Boolean operators between terms: "AND," "OR," and "NOT." Example: Drug AND Enforcement

All Word Search: Locates articles that include all terms in an article. Drug Enforcement = Drug AND Enforcement with the Standard Word Search option.

Any Word Search: Looks for any of the search terms in an article. Drug Enforcement = Drug OR Enforcement with the Standard Word Search Option.

Exact Phrase Search: Searches for an exact phrase like "The Rise and Fall of."

Activity

A. Perform a Standard Word Search on [Drug Enforcement] in the Criminal Justice database.

How many articles are retrieved?

B. Perform a Standard Word Search on [Drug AND Enforcement] in the Criminal Justice Database.

How many articles are retrieved?

You have to make sure to put one of the Boolean expressions between terms with the Standard Word Search.

C. Perform a search on [The Rise and Fall of] in the Criminal Justice Database with the "Exact phrase" option. Do not enclose the phrase in quotation marks.

How many articles are retrieved?

Selecting Multiple Databases

You can perform a multiple database search by pressing the [Alt] or [Command] keys when making your database selections in ContentSelect from the Research Navigator homepage.

The *New York Times* Archive search has an option for selecting all subject categories. You could manually select all categories with Content Select. But because ContentSelect is much larger and includes academic journals with technical research, it is more efficient to limit the number of databases you select. It does though often make sense to select two or more databases for a single search.

Activity

A. Select two databases from the ContentSelect search window: "Criminal Justice" and "Sociology," then enter the keyword: "gangs."

How many articles did ContentSelect retrieve?

Advanced Selecting and De-selecting a Database. To de-select a database, click on the "**Choose Database**" tab. A hyperlinked list of all the databases appears. From here you can add or delete the databases of your choice. You can select a single database by simply clicking on the title-link of the

database title of your choosing. For multiple database selections, click on the title box beside the database titles. A checkmark will appear in the box alongside the database you have selected during your current search. To de-select, simply erase the check mark by clicking on it in the database title box.

Activity
A. De-select the Sociology database.
When you search the keyword "Gangs" with only the Criminal Justice database, how many articles do you get? What are some of the other ContentSelect databases that might have articles about gangs, in addition to the "Criminal Justice" and "Sociology" databases?

Exploring the Databases. For each discipline, ContentSelect usually contains 50-100 of the leading academic journals. The Criminal Justice section has only 15 journals. However, the "General Interest" collection includes over 150 titles, many of them related to criminal justice. The FBI Law Enforcement Bulletin, for example, appears under the "General" category.

In addition, news publications with a strong public policy focus like *National Review*, *The Nation*, *Reason*, and the *New Amsterdam News* frequently include stories with a law enforcement theme.

Databases like "Communications," "Education," "Psychology," and others include publications and articles pertinent to topics in criminal justice research.

Title List (Publications). If you click on the "Title List" link that appears under each Database, in "Choose Database," you can view a list of every publication that provides articles for your searches in a selected database.

If you put a checkmark in the title box beside a publication and press "search," ContentSelect will retrieve every article in the database from that particular publication. Articles appear in chronological order with articles from the most recent issue appearing first.

Clicking on a title in the list returns some general information about the publication and a URL for its Web page if applicable. The Publications button that appears on the line below "Choose Database" provides the exact same information and functionality as the Title List links found in "Choose Database."

Activity
A. Click on the title "Criminal Justice Policy Review."
How frequently does this publication come out? How much is an annual subscription?
B. Place a check next to "Criminal Justice Policy Review" and press "Search."
What is the most recent issue in the ContentSelect Database for this title?

Searching Individual Publications. When you do a search of all the articles from a particular journal in the database, you may observe that the search window has generated and placed the following text in the search window: **(JN "Criminal Justice Policy Review")**.

Manually performing this search using the same or a simpler syntax **[SO Criminal Justice Policy Review]** retrieves all articles from this journal in the Criminal Justice Database. **[AU Innes, Martin]** retrieves all articles in the Criminal Justice database by author Martin Innes.

When performing an author search you must put the last name first. A first name is not required.

Activity
A. Do a publication search on the *Christian Science Monitor* in the General Interest database.
How many articles appear on the list?
From the same database, do an author search on "Howard Fineman."
What is the first article that appears on the list?

You *usually* do not have to include the first name of an author. If the author's name is a common name such as "George Will," you might need to include a first name also.

Searching Individual Publications for Specific Topics. You can
also search an individual publication on a particular topic. Using the Standard Word option in the General Interest category you can search *Newsweek Magazine* for articles about Juvenile Violence with the following search:
  [SO Newsweek AND Juvenile AND Violence]
You can search the *Christian Science Monitor* for articles about Drug Enforcement with the search:
  [SO Christian Science Monitor AND Drug AND Enforcement]
Note: You do not have to include the Boolean "AND" between the names of publications or authors even when using the Standard Word search option.

To look up articles about baseball in *Newsweek Magazine* by author George Will enter:
  [SO Newsweek AND AU will, george AND baseball]
You cannot do these more advanced searches from the ContentSelect search utility on the Research Navigator homepage. There are other limitations with the ContentSelect "keyword" search from the homepage as well. For more complex searches it is better to work from the results page.

Other Searchable Parameters. In addition to Author, "AU," and
Publication, "SO," these are some other search macros you can use for retrieving results:

TI	Title
SU	Subject
AB	Abstract
AN	Accession Number
IS	ISSN
AS	Author Supplied Abstract

Abstracts and Full Texts. ContentSelect retrieves two kinds of results, "Abstracts" and "Full Texts." Abstracts only have a summary of the article, and citation information that will help you retrieve the full text of the article from a library or other source. Full Text results provide citation information as well as the full text of the entire article for online viewing, printing, or saving.

Retrieving Full Text Only. You can limit results to only full text by clicking on the tab "Advanced Search" and clicking the box "Full Text." Once you limit your searches in this way, the phrase "Limiters Set" appears in red letters above the Refine Search box just above your results. If you click on "Refine Search" you can remove the check next to "Full Text," and will again have both Abstract and Full Text results.

Looking at Individual Results. If you perform a search on "Burglary" in the Criminal Justice Database, one of the results should be:

Mapping an Opportunity Surface of Residential Burglary.; By: Groff, Elizabeth R.; La Vigne, Nancy G.., Journal of Research in Crime & Delinquency, Aug2001, Vol. 38 Issue 3, p257, 22p, 1 diagram, 1 graph, 2 maps
HTML Full Text **PDF Full Text** **(131K)**

Clicking on **HTML Full Text** **PDF Full Text** provides a full of view the article.

If you click on the title link:

Mapping an Opportunity Surface of Residential Burglary

you can view information about the article, the publisher, and other links to related searches.

If you click on any of the links in the subject line:

Subject(s): CRIME forecasting; COMPUTER software; BURGLARY; CRIMINOLOGY

ContentSelect will automatically perform a search on the subject area you selected.

Source: **Journal of Research in Crime & Delinquency,**
Aug2001, Vol. 38 Issue 3, p257, 22p, 1 diagram, 1 graph, 2 maps

Clicking on the source provides general information about the Publication and a link to its Web page if applicable.

Author(s): Groff, Elizabeth R.; La Vigne, Nancy G.

You can perform an author search by clicking on the author links automatically generated along with each article.

> **Abstract:** The use of geographic information systems (GIS) to understand spatial patterns of crime etc....
> [ABSTRACT FROM AUTHOR]

The abstract provides a brief summary of the article, often written by the author.

> **Other Information provided.**
> AN: 5046449
> ISSN: 0022-4278
> Full Text Word Count: 7713
> Database: ContentSelect Criminal Justice

This information and accompanying links can help with subsequent searches, so it may not always be advisable to limit your searches to Full Texts. You might, through an author link from an Abstract result, locate a full text article on the same topic by that author.

Result Preferences. From the **"Preferences"** button in the upper right-hand corner of the page, you can adjust the order and manner in which ContentSelect returns results.

ContentSelect normally displays the first ten articles found for your search. However, if you click the "Preferences" button in the upper right hand corner of the page, you can adjust the number of results displayed from 5 to 50. Click on the number of results you want to display and hit "Apply." ContentSelect re-executes the search with the new parameters. However, adjustments made in "Preferences" are not permanent. When you make your next search, the system will revert to the default setting of ten articles automatically.

From "Preferences" you can also temporarily adjust how the results are displayed. The default setting provides the title and a brief description. You can adjust the display, however, to only include the title. You can also select the option "Detailed," which will provide not only the article title, but also the entire abstract of the article.

The "Sort" option permits you to adjust the results from the default setting to one that lists the results alphabetically either by publication or by author's last name. The Sort default displays results based on the frequency that a term appears in the text. Not all Databases have the Author Sort, including the Criminal Justice Database.

Activity

A. Perform a search on Juvenile AND Violence with the General Interest Database, using the Standard Word option.
What article appears first in the returned list?
What article appears first with the same search if you adjust the search under Preferences, so that "Source" is selected with the "Sort" Option?

The Filter option enables you to select a single database for a single search by filtering out the results of other databases you have selected. This saves you the time and effort of deselecting databases and then adding them back in.

Activity

A. Do a search of the Databases Criminal Justice, General Interest, and Sociology.
How many articles does ContentSelect Retrieve?
If you select the Sociology database in the Filter option under Preferences, how many articles does ContentSelect return?

Saving Your Results

Your results list-display includes a small folder icon with the word "added" below. There is one folder for every result displayed on the right-hand side of the page. Clicking on the folder will store the results for later use. The master-folder where all the saved documents you select are kept appears just to the right of the Search window. The folder also keeps a running tally of the number of items stored in the folder.

The master-folder provides a convenient place for storing potentially useful resources while pressing forward with your research. From this storage folder, you can view your saved results. It also provides convenient methods to print, save-to-disk (or your computer's hard drive), remove, or e-mail the documents. You have to open Adobe pdf documents in order to save them.

Targeted Internet Searching with Link Library

Research Navigator's **Link Library** provides access to the most informative and authoritative Web pages in numerous academic disciplines. Thousands of links are organized by subject area, including "Criminal Justice." Research Navigator's editors search websites for hundreds of course-specific terms. Links to the most suitable sites are then added to Link Library and organized by key concepts.

Link Library will keep your research focused on relevant subject matter by eliminating time wasted on lengthy or dead-end site searches, and give you more time to explore worthwhile sites.

You can access Link Library resources by selecting a subject in the *search window* under the Link Library logo. Just highlight a subject with the arrow key and click on the "Go" button.

In addition to the Criminal Justice area, the other subject categories contain numerous resources that should be of interest to Criminal Justice researchers. In the category **Decision Science–Project Management**, for example, there is a topic area called "Active Listening." One of the links in this category is to a paper from the FBI called "Using Active Listening Skills in a Crisis Situation." It describes how FBI negotiators use active listening skills during a crisis to help evaluate the situation and resolve it quickly.

Activity
A. What are some of the other subject areas you can access from the Research Navigator homepage in Link Library that pertain to Criminal Justice research? (Choose 3)
Find a topic area within each of the three subjects you selected that would be relevant to the study of Criminal Justice.
Find a link within each of the topic areas you selected that you believe would be especially useful.

The Criminal Justice Subject Area of the Link Library
The Criminal Justice section includes over 500 Web pages and documents organized into about 90 distinct topic areas.

In addition to the links, each topic page includes a definition of its "key concept": deviant behavior, the death penalty, DNA, drug abuse, etc. The topic area "Roman Law," for example, includes the definition: "Body of law derived from the Twelve Tablets (450 B.C.) that guided governance of ancient Rome."

Activity
A. How is Money Laundering defined on that topic page?
What other helpful information is found in the header above the display of resource links?

Locating Resources
Research Navigator's links are organized alphabetically. For your convenience, this guide includes a list of all categories.

Activity
A. Under which topic areas in the Criminal Justice section would you look to find information on a suspect's Fifth Amendment Right against self-incrimination? (List 4)

B. What topic areas would be helpful for a research project on juvenile violent crime? (List 5)

Different Views of Link Library Resources

Another way to access the Criminal Justice section of Link Library is with the following link:

http://navigator:access@www.pearsoncustom.com/link/candt/cj/cj/

From this link you can view the alphabetized list of links, just as you do via the search window from the Research Navigator homepage. But you can also view the links divided into five broad categories:

Courts/Adjudication
Crime
Criminal Law
Policing
Sentencing/Corrections

You can also view all of the subject areas in the Link Library database on a single page rather than scrolling from the search window on the Research Navigator homepage:

http://navigator:access@www.pearsoncustom.com/link/index.html

Accessing the subject areas from this page allows you the option of selecting from the broad categories *or* the alphabetized list of all links after you select a subject discipline (i.e., Biology, Sociology).

Activity

A. In the American Government section under Political Science/American Government, do you think it is better to pick from one or two of the broad categories, or to view the entire alphabetized list?

Which two of the broad categories under Political Science/American Government would be most helpful for a student of Criminal Justice?

Research Navigator LINK LIBRARY
CRIMINAL JUSTICE—
DIRECTORY OF CATEGORIES

Access All Subject Areas
http://navigator:access@www.pearsoncustom.com/link/index.html

Access Criminal Justice by Topic
http://navigator:access@www.pearsoncustom.com/link/candt/cj/cj/

Index of All Criminal Justice Categories

Sentencing (includes consecutive, concurrent, mandatory)	U.S. Constitution
	UCR Program

Subpoenas

Suicide

White-Collar Crime

Women in Prison

Terrorism

Treason (includes espionage)

Criminal Justice Web Portal: The Prentice Hall Cybrary

One of the best online resources for Criminal Justice Research is the Prentice Hall Cybrary at http://www.cybrary.info. With over 12,000 links, the Prentice Hall Cybrary is one of the leading portal sites in any subject area, and is an indispensable online tool for Criminal Justice research.

Top 100 Picks

A good place to familiarize yourself with the Prentice Hall Cybrary is the Top 100 Picks page. The Top 100 includes links to all of the leading sites in the Criminal Justice field in areas such as research, education, employment, and law. The following is sample of the excellent sites to be found here:

Atlantic Monthly's Criminology Collection
http://www.theatlantic.com/election/connection/crime/crime.htm

Corrections Connection
http://www.corrections.com

National Institute of Justice International Center
http://www.ojp.usdoj.gov/nij/international/

Browse Index

To get a sense of the depth and scope of the Cybrary, click on the "Browse Index" link. There are nearly 150 categories. The Death Penalty category has dozens of links, the Associations category has hundreds of links, the Government Publications category has over 2000 links! The links are an updated archive of government documents related to Criminal Justice research, statistics, projections, plans, and programs.

Activity

A. About how many documents in the Government Publications section concern Gangs?
Reminder: You can search through the list by using Edit, Find [or Ctrl + F] to find key terms like "gang."

Browsing the Government Documents category is one way to survey the research terrain on a given topic. Looking at the titles you can learn related terminology and topics to help perform other searches. In reports with the word "Gang" in the title, for example, there are reports about the extent of gang involvement in various locations, contributing factors to gang involvement, community solutions to the problem, and law enforcement's response to gang criminal activity.

Cybrary Search Engine

The real key to the Prentice Hall Cybrary is the Cybrary search engine. The site search engine enables you to quickly and conveniently access and navigate through this enormous collection of well-maintained links. You create your own "categories" by the search engine terms you select.

Search Engine Syntax.

1. The Cybrary search engine only searches the title block of the description. If you searched the word "methamphetamine," and that word appears in the description of a website but *not* in the title, then the search engine will not return the document with the results of your search.

2. The search engine looks for *all* of the words you enter by default. If you enter:

   [Journal Letter Health]

   The Cybrary search returns: "Forensic Panel Letter - Journal on Forensics and Mental Health," and only this link because this is the only resource in the Cybrary that has the words "Journal" and "Letter" and "Health" in the title.

3. You can put the Boolean term "OR" into the search so that the Cybrary search engine looks for Journal OR Letter OR Health.

4. The Cybrary does not support the Boolean Term "NOT."

5. You can limit the results by enclosing terms in quotation marks. The search:

   [Drug Court]

   would include "Drug Offense Cases in Juvenile Courts, 1989–1998. 2001." The search: **["Drug Court"]** would *not* include this document. While the words "Drug" and "Court" both appear in the title, they do not appear side by side. The search, **["Drug Court"]** looks for the exact phrase in the title.

Activity

A. How many results are returned from the Cybrary search engine for the search [Drug Court]?

How many from [Drug OR Court]?

How many from ["Drug Court"]?

Advanced Search. The advanced search option lets you adjust the number of returns you view at any one time. The default setting is ten, but from Advanced Search you can change the number of results to 50, 100, or All. This can be a handy option when you have a large number of results and you want to scan through them quickly.

Research Navigator
Frequently Asked Questions

EBSCO's Content Select
What is "Standard Word Search" on Ebsco Content Select?
The Standard Word Search option recognizes and requires one of the Boolean operators between terms: "AND," "OR," or "NOT." It is the default setting for ContentSelect from the Research Navigator homepage.

How do I De-Select a database with ContentSelect?
To de-select a database, you click on the "**Choose Database**" tab. A hyperlinked list of all the databases appears. From here you can add or delete the database(s) of your choice.

How can I view the Title List of publications for each database?
If you click on the "Title List" link that appears under each database, in "Choose Database," you can view a list of every publication that provides articles for your searches within a selected database.

How can I view all of the articles in the publication *Criminal Justice Policy Review*?
You must first ensure that "Criminal Justice" is one of the databases you have already selected, since *Criminal Justice Policy Review* resides in that database. Then enter:
    [SO Criminal Justice Policy Review]

How can I view all of the articles that George Will has written about baseball in *Newsweek Magazine* that are available?
You must first ensure that "General Interest" is one of the databases you have already selected since *Newsweek* resides in that database, then enter:
    [SO Newsweek AND AU will, george AND baseball]

How can I limit my results to only Full Text documents?
You can limit results to only full text by clicking on the tab "Advanced Search" and clicking the box "Full Text." Once you limit your searches in this way, the phrase "Limiters Set" appears in red letters above the Refine Search box just above your results. If you click on "Refine Search" you can remove the check next to "Full Text," and will again have both Abstract and Full Text results.

The *New York Times* Archive
In searching the *New York Times* Archive, how do I retrieve results with the most recent articles first?
Select the "Time" Option under "Sort By" above the search window. The "Reverse Time" option sorts results so that the oldest articles appear first.

How do I perform a keyword search in the *New York Times* Archive within one of the subjects listed on the homepage?
From the Research Navigator homepage, you can either perform a keyword search of all subjects, or retrieve all of the articles within a subject. You cannot do both.

From the results page, however, you can combine keyword and subject searches. To search for articles about "DNA" within the Criminal Law subject area enter:

[SubjectCriminalLaw dna]

Can you perform Boolean searches of the *New York Times* Archive?
Yes, when you search from the Research Navigator homepage, the default setting on a keyword search is "Any." In Boolean terminology a search from the Research Navigator homepage of [police dna evidence] = [police OR dna OR evidence]

If you select "All" in the "Match" options, it is the equivalent of the AND command in Boolean syntax. [police dna evidence] with "All" = [police AND dna AND evidence] with Boolean.

You can also select the Boolean option under "Match" which allows you to add the NOT command.

[Cardinals NOT baseball NOT football]
Or to combine Boolean commands:

[police AND investigation OR evidence NOT dna]

Prentice Hall Cybrary
What is the URL for the Prentice Hall Cybrary?
The Prentice Hall Cybrary can be found at http://www.cybrary.info.

What is the default setting on the Cybrary Search Engine?
The search engine returns links in the Cybrary that have *all* of the terms in the title of a document or Web page that were entered into the search engine. To perform a search for any of the words in your search, you must put "OR" between the words.

Link Library
What is the URL for the page that includes All Subject Areas in the Link Library?
   http://navigator:access@www.pearsoncustom.com/link/index.html

General Navigation Commands
What is the command for locating a particular term or phrase within a document?
   [Ctrl + F]

What is the command for moving from one open window or document to another on my browser?
    [Ctrl + Tab]

What is the command for returning to the top of a document?
    [Ctrl + Home]

What is the Internet browser command for going directly to my Home Page?
    [Alt + Home]

What if I just want to start over without logging off from Research Navigator?
Click on the Home tab, which appears at the top center of every Research Navigator page.

Appendix A

Documenting Your Electronic Sources

Copyright laws came into effect when people started realizing that income could be made by selling their words. In an era dubbed "The Age of Information," knowledge and words are taking on more significance than ever. Laws requiring writers to document or give credit to the sources of their information, while evolving, are still in effect.

Various organizations have developed style manuals detailing, among other style matters, how to document sources in their particular disciplines. For writing in English composition and literature, Modern Language Association (MLA) and American Psychological Association (APA) guidelines are the most commonly used, but others, such as those in *The Chicago Manual of Style* (CMS), are available. Always find out from your instructor what style to use in a specific assignment so that you can follow the appropriate guidelines.

For general information on MLA and APA citations, the best print sources are:

> Gibaldi, Joseph. MLA Handbook for Writers of Research Papers. 5th ed. NY: MLA, 1999.

> American Psychological Association. (2001). *Publication Manual of the American Psychological Association* (5th ed.). Washington: APA.

Because the methods of obtaining electronic information are developing so rapidly, printed style manuals have had difficulty in keeping up with the changes and in developing documentation styles for electronic sources. As a result, the most up-to-date information from the MLA and the APA about documenting online sources with URLs can be found on these organizations' websites. This Appendix shows you how to credit your electronic sources based on the information there.

When you cite electronic sources, it is vital to type every letter, number, symbol, and space accurately. Any error makes it impossible to retrieve your source. Since electronic sources tend to be transitory, printing a hard copy of your sources will make it easier for you to cite accurately and provide evidence for your documentation. MLA style encloses Internet addresses and URLs (Uniform Resource Locators) in angle brackets < >. If you see them around an address, do not use them as part of the address when you attempt to retrieve the source. APA style does not enclose URLs.

Modern Language Association (MLA) Style Guidelines

These guidelines follow the documentation style authorized by the Modern Language Association for electronic sources. Web sources are documented in basically the same way as traditional sources. According to the MLA website, the following items should be included if they are available:

1. Name of the author, editor, compiler, or translator of the source (if available and relevant), reversed for alphabetizing and followed by an abbreviation, such as ed., if appropriate
2. Title of a poem, short story, article, or similar short work within a scholarly project, database, or periodical (in quotation marks); or title of a posting to a discussion list or forum (taken from the subject line and put in quotation marks), followed by the description Online posting
3. Title of a book (underlined)
4. Name of the editor, compiler, or translator of the text (if relevant and if not cited earlier), preceded by the appropriate abbreviation, such as ed.
5. Publication information for any print version of the source
6. Title of the scholarly project, database, periodical, or professional or personal site (underlined); or, for a professional or personal site with no title, a description such as Homepage
7. Name of the editor of the scholarly project or database (if available)
8. Version number of the source (if not part of the title) or, for a journal, the volume number, issue number, or other identifying number
9. Date of electronic publication, of the latest update, or of posting
10. For a posting to a discussion list or forum, the name of the list or forum
11. The number range or total number of pages, paragraphs, or other sections, if they are numbered
12. Name of any institution or organization sponsoring or associated with the website
13. Date when the researcher accessed the source
14. Electronic address, or URL, of the source (in angle brackets)

Examples:

Book
Shaw, Bernard. <u>Pygmalion</u>. 1912. Bartleby Archive. 6
    Mar. 1998 <http://www.columbia.edu/acis/
    bartleby/shaw/>.

Poem

Carroll, Lewis. "Jabberwocky." 1872. 6 Mar. 1998.
    <http://www.jabberwocky.com/carroll/jabber/
    jabberwocky.html>.

Article in a Journal

Rehberger, Dean. "The Censoring of Project #17:
    Hypertext Bodies and Censorship." Kairos 2.2
    (Fall 1997): 14 secs. 6 Mar. 1998 <http://
    english.ttu.edu/kairos/2.2/index_f.html>.

Article in a Magazine

Viagas, Robert, and David Lefkowitz. "Capeman Closing
    Mar. 28." Playbill 5 Mar. 1998. 6 Mar. 1998
    <http://www1.playbill.com/cgi-bin/plb/news?cmd
    =show&code=30763>.

Article in a Newspaper

Sandomir, Richard. "Yankees Talk Trades in Broadcast
    Booth." New York Times on the Web 4 Dec. 2001. 5
    Dec. 2001 <http://www.nytimes.com/pages/
    business/media/index.html>.

Article in a Reference Database

"Jupiter." Britannica Online. Vers. 97.1.1 Mar. 1997.
    Encyclopaedia Britannica. 29 Mar. 1998 <http://
    www.eb.com:180>.

Posting to a Discussion List

Grumman, Bob. "Shakespeare's Literacy." Online
    posting. 6 Mar. 1998. Deja News. <humanities.
    lit.author>.

Scholarly Project

Voice of the Shuttle: Web Page for Humanities
    Research. Ed. Alan Liu. Mar. 1998. U of
    California Santa Barbara. 8 Mar. 1998
    <http://humanitas.ucsb.edu/>.

Professional Site

The Nobel Foundation Official Website. The Nobel
    Foundation. 28 Feb. 1998 <http://www.nobel.se/>.

Personal Site

Thiroux, Emily. Home page. 7 Mar. 1998
    <http://academic.csubak.edu/home/acadpro/
    departments/english/engthrx.htmlx>.

Government or Institutional Site

Zebra Mussels in Vermont. Homepage. State of Vermont
    Agency of Natural Resources. 3 May 1998 <http://
    www.anr.state.vt.us/dec/waterq/smcap.htm>.

Synchronous Communications (such as MOOs, MUDs, and IRCs)

Ghostly Presence. Group Discussion. telnet 16 Mar.
    1997 <moo.du.org:8000/80anon/anonview/1
    4036#focus>.

Gopher Sites

Banks, Vickie, and Joe Byers. "EDTECH." 18 Mar. 1997
    <gopher://ericyr.syr.edu:70/00/Listservs/EDTECH/
    README>.

FTP (File Transfer Protocol) Sites

U.S. Supreme Court directory. 6 Mar. 1998
    <ftp://ftp.cwru.edu/U.S.Supreme.Court/>.

Online Work of Art

Van Gogh, Vincent. The Olive Trees. 1889. Museum of
    Modern Art, New York. 5 Dec. 2001 <http://
    www.moma.org/docs/collection/paintsculpt/
    recent/c463.htm>.

Online Interview

Plaxco, Jim. Interview. Planetary Studies Foundation.
    Oct. 1992. 5 Dec. 2001 <http://www.planets.org>.

Online Film or Film Clip

Columbus, Chris, dir. Harry Potter and the Sorcerer's
    Stone. Trailer. Warner Brothers, 2001. 5 Dec.
    2001 <http://hollywood.com>.

Electronic Television or Radio Program

Chayes, Sarah. "Concorde." All Things Considered.
    Natl. Public Radio. 26 July 2000. 7 Dec. 2001
    <http://www.npr.com/programs/atc/archives>.

Synchronous Communication

Author's last name, First name. Identifying label.
    "Title of work." xx Month 20xx. Name of forum.
    xx Month 20xx. <Telnet://lingua.networkname>.

Generally follow the guidelines for other online citations, modifying them
wherever necessary, but always provide as much information as possible. Some
cited material will require identifying labels (e.g., Interview or Online posting),
but such labels should be neither underlined nor set within quotation marks.
When documenting synchronous communications that are posted in MOO
(multiuser domain, object oriented) and MUD (multiuser domain) forums, name

the speaker or speakers; describe the event; provide the date of the event and the name of the forum (e.g., linguaMOO); and cite the date of access as well as the network name (including the prefix Telnet://).

Work from an Online Service

```
Author's last name, First name. Publication. 20xx.
     Internet Provider name. xx Month 20xx. Keyword:
     Name.
```

Or

```
Last name, First name. Publication. 20xx. Internet
     Provider name. xx Month 20xx. Path: Name; Name;
     Name.
```

```
Brash, Stephen B. "Bioprospecting the Public Domain."
     Cultural Anthropology 14.4 (1999): 535-56.
     ProQuest Direct. Teaneck Public Library,
     Teaneck, NJ. 7 Dec. 1999 <http://proquest.
     umi.com>.
```

Or

```
Dutton, Gail. "Greener Pigs." Popular Science 255.5
     (1999): 38-39. ProQuest Direct. Teaneck Public
     Library, Teaneck, NJ. 7 Dec. 1999 <http://
     proquest.umi.com>.
```

For works that have been accessed through an online service, either through a library service (e.g., ProQuest Direct or Lexis-Nexis) or through one of the large Internet providers (e.g., America Online), you may not know the URL of the source. In such cases, cite the keyword or path that led to the source, if applicable, and separate each individual item in the path with a semicolon; the keyword or path will be the last item in the citation. For sources accessed through library services, as above, cite the name of the service, the name of the library, the date you assessed the material, and the URL of the service's homepage. If you also know the name of the database used, include that information (underlined) before the name of the online service.

American Psychological Association (APA) Style Guidelines

The most recent (5th) edition of the *Publication Manual of the American Psychological Association* includes general guidelines for citing electronic sources, and the APA has published specific examples for documenting Web sources on its Web page. Go to:

http://www.apastyle.org/elecre.html

In general, document these sources as you do traditional sources, giving credit to the author and including the title and date of publication. Include as much information as possible to help your reader to be able to retrieve the information. Any sources that are not generally available to your readers should be documented within the body of your writing as a personal communication but not included in your reference list. Such sources include material from listservs, newsgroups, Internet relay chats (IRCs), MOOs, MUDs, and e-mail.

According to information at the website for the American Psychological Association entitled "How to Cite Information From the World Wide Web," all references begin with the same information that would be provided for a printed source (or as much of that information as possible). The Web information is then placed at the end of the reference. It is important to use the "Retrieved from" and the date because documents on the Web may change in content, move, or be removed from a site altogether. To cite a website in text (but not a specific document), it's sufficient to give the address (e.g., http://www.apa.org) there. No reference entry is needed.

Use the following guidelines to include a source in your reference list:

```
Name of author [if given]. (Publication date) [in
    parentheses]. Title of the article [following
    APA guidelines for capitalization]. Title of
    periodical or electronic text [italicized].
    Volume number and/or pages [if any]. Retrieved
    [include the date here] from the World Wide Web:
    [include the URL here, and do not end with a
    period]
```

Examples:

Journal Article
```
Fine, M. A. & Kurdek, L. A. (1993, November).
    Reflections on determining authorship credit and
    authorship order on faculty-student
    collaborations. American Psychologist, 48.11,
    1141-1147. Retrieved March 6, 1998 from the
    World Wide Web: http://www.apa.org/journals/
    amp/kurdek.html
```

Newspaper Article
```
Murray, B. (1998, February). Email bonding with your
    students. APA Monitor [Newspaper, selected
    stories online]. Retrieved March 6, 1998 from
    the World Wide Web: http://www.apa.org/monitor/
    bond.html
```

World Wide Web Site
Williams, Scott. (1996, June 14). Back to school
    with the quilt. *AIDS Memorial Quilt Website*.
    Retrieved June 14, 1996, from http://www.
    aidsquilt.org/newsletter/stoires/backto.html

File Transfer Protocol (FTP), Telnet, or Gopher Site
Altar, T.W. (1993). *Vitamin B12 and vegans*. Retrieved
    May 28, 1996, from ftp://ftp.cs.yle.edu

King, Jr., M.L. (1963, August 28). I have a dream
    [speech]. Retrieved January 2, 1996, from
    telnet://ukanaix.cc.ukans.edu

Synchronous Communications (MOO, MUD, IRC)
Harnack, A. (1996, April 4). Words [Group
    discussion]. Retrieved April 5, 1996, from
    telnet://moo.du.org/port=8888

Web Discussion Forum
Holden, J.B. (2001, January 2). The failure of higher
    education [Formal discussion initiation].
    Message posted to http://ifets.mtu.edu/archives

Listserv (electronic mailing list)
Weston, Heather (2002, June 12). Re: Registration
    schedule now available. Message posted to the
    Chamberlain Kronsage dormitory electronic
    mailing list, archived at http://listserv.
    registrar.uwsp.edu/archives/62.html

Newsgroup
Hotgirl (2002, January 12). Dowsing effort fails.
    Message posted to news://alt.science.esp3/html

Appendix B

Glossary

Boolean Comes from the ideas of British mathematician George Boole (1815-1964). From his writings come the Boolean operators: AND, OR, and NOT, used to link words and phrases for more precise queries for search engines and directories.

Database A repository of information that is searchable.

Domain One of the different subsets of the Internet. The suffix found on the host name of an Internet server defines its domain. For example, the host name for Prentice Hall, the publisher of this book, is www.prenhall.com. The last part, .COM, indicates that Prentice Hall is a part of the commercial domain. Other domains include .MIL for military, .EDU for education, .ORG for non-profit organizations, .GOV for government organizations, and many more.

Download The process of transferring a file, document, or program from a remote computer to a local computer. (See Upload.)

E-mail The short name for electronic mail. E-mail is sent electronically from one person to another. Some companies have e-mail systems that are not part of the Internet. E-mail can be sent to one person or to many different people.

Homepage In its specific sense, this refers to a Web document that a browser loads as its central navigational point to browse the Internet. It may also be used to refer to as a Web page describing an individual. In the most general sense, it is used to refer to any Web document.

Host Another name for a server computer. (See Server.)

HTML This is an abbreviation for HyperText Markup Language, the common language used to write documents that appear on the World Wide Web.

HTTP An abbreviation for HyperText Transport Protocol, the common protocol used to communicate between World Wide Web servers.

Link A text element or graphic within a document that has an embedded connection to another item. Web pages use links to access documents, images, sounds, and video files from the Internet, other documents on the local Web server, or other content on the Web page. Hyperlink is another name for link.

Multimedia As a general definition, multimedia is the presentation of information by multiple media formats, such as words, images, and sound. Today, it is more commonly used to refer to presentations that use a lot of computer technology.

Nesting The use of parentheses to combine several search statements into one search statement.

Paraphrasing To restate in your own words a passage written or spoken by another person.

PDF This stands for Portable Document Format. It is a file format that allows authors to distribute formatted, high-resolution documents across the Internet. A free viewer, Adobe Acrobat Reader, is required to view PDF documents.

Plagiarism To present another person's words or ideas as if they were your own.

Primary Source Firsthand evidence, based on your own or someone else's original work or direct observation.

Search Engine An online service or utility that enables users to query and search the Internet for user-defined information. They are typically free services to the user.

Secondary Source To report describe, comment or analyze the experiences of work of others. A secondary source is at least once removed from the primary source.

Server A software program used to provide, or serve, information to remote computers. Servers function in a Client-Server information exchange model. This term may also be loosely applied to the computer that is used to serve the information.

Summarizing To condense the essentials of someone else's thoughts into a few statements. A summary is shorter than a paraphrase and provides only the main point from the original source.

Truncate To use a root of a word followed by an asterisk in order to retrieve variants of the word.

Upload The process of moving or transferring a document, file, or program from one computer to another computer.

URL An abbreviation for Universal Resource Locator. It is basic sense, it is an address used by people on the Internet to locate documents. URLs have a common format that describes the protocol for information transfer, the host computer address, the path to the desired file, and the name of the file requested.

Viewer A program used to view data files within or outside a browser.

Web (WWW) This stands for World Wide Web. When loosely applied, this term refers to the Internet and all of its associated incarnations, including Gopher, FTP, HTTP, and others. More specifically, this term refers to a subset of the servers on the Internet that use HTTP to transfer hyperlinked documents in a page-like format.

Web page A single file as viewed within a Web browser. Sever Web pages linked together represent a website.

References

Chapter 1

Barstow, D., & Bergman, L. (2003, January 9). A family's fortune, a legacy of blood and tears. *The New York Times*, p. A1.

Holland, E.I.M., Ph.D. (1997). *From the Mississippi Delta: A Memoir.* New York: Simon & Schuster.

Troyka, L.Q. (2002). *Simon & Schuster Handbook for Writers* (6th ed.). Upper Saddle River, NJ: Pearson Education.

Chapter 2

The Basics of Google Search. (2002). Retrieved February 27, 2003, from http://www.google.com/help/refinesearch.html

Finding Information on the Internet: A Tutorial. (2002). Retrieved January 14, 2003, from http://www.lib.berkeley.edu/TeachingLib/Guides/Internet/Strategies.html

Gallagher, D. F. (2002, December 9). In the 'Google' economy,' businesses thrive by appearing prominently on the search engine's free listings. *The New York Times*, p. E1.

Global Warming: Fact vs. Myth. (2001). Retrieved March 3, 2003, from http://www.environmentaldefense.org/documents/382_myths.htm

Internet Searching Tools. (2002). Retrieved February 27, 2003, from http://www.sou.edu/library/searchtools

Searching FAQs. (2003). Retrieved February 26, 2003, from http://www.cln.org/searching_faqs.html

Sullivan, D. (2001, October 26). Search engine math. *Search Engine Watch*. Retrieved January 13, 2003, from http://searchenginewatch.com/facts/math.html

Cohen, L. B. (2003). Internet tutorials. *University at Albany Libraries*. Retrieved January 11, 2003, from http://library.albany.edu/internet

Whalen, J. (2002, October 30). Explaining the recent Yahoo/Google changes. *Traffick.com*. Retrieved February 26, 2003, from http://www.traffick.com/article.asp?aID=120

Chapter 3

Chokshi, M., Carter, C., Gupta, D., Martin, T., & Allen, R. (1991). Computers and the apartheid regime in South Africa. *South Africa. Guide to Internet Resources. Stanford University*. Retrieved Dec. 12, 2002, from http://www-cs-students.stanford.edu/~cale/cs201

Goldstein, N. (Ed.). (1998) *The Associated Press Stylebook and Libel Manual*. Reading, MA: Addison-Wesley.

Halberstam, D. (2002, May 20). A Pultizer Prize-winner speaks of terrorism, life after college and choosing wisely. *USC Chronicle, 21*(29), 10-11.

Sollee, D. (2001). *Smart Marriages. The Coalition for Marriage, Family and Couples Education*. Retrieved December 12, 2002, from http://www.smartmarriages.com/divorcepredictor.html

Troyka, L.Q. (2002). *Simon & Schuster Handbook for Writers* (6th ed.). Upper Saddle River, NJ: Pearson Education.

Chapter 5

New York Times Newspaper 2001 Fact Book. (2003). Retrieved February 16, 2003, from http://www.nytco.com/company-factbook.html

Chapter 7

Evarts, E. C. (2000, July 6). Gas-guzzling SUVs muster up a makeover. *Christian Science Monitor*.